ROYA
PRINCE ANDREW

This is the first definitive account of the courtship
and marriage of H.R.H. Prince Andrew and Miss
Sarah Ferguson. In writing it journalist Tim
Satchell has drawn upon exclusive and original
material to give us the full inside story of their
romance. The book traces the early days of their
childhood friendship right through to the
magnificent Royal Wedding day, and provides
fascinating insights into the characters of these
two little-known people. Complete with colour
pictures of the wedding, ROYAL ROMANCE
will stand as a wonderful memento of a very
special occasion.

C000278825

About the Author

Tim Satchell is a journalist who has written for the *Daily Express*, *Sunday Express*, *The Times*, *Daily Mail*, and other newspapers and magazines on showbusiness, personalities and the Royal Family. He has written a biography of Steve McQueen and a soon-to-be-published definitive work on Fred Astaire.

His London house is a few hundred yards from Buckingham Palace, where he lives with his wife, Amanda, one year old daughter, Cordelia, and Golden Cocker Spaniel, Blondie.

Royal Romance Prince Andrew and Sarah Ferguson

Tim Satchell

NEW ENGLISH LIBRARY
Hodder and Stoughton

Copyright © 1986 by Tim Satchell

First published in 1986 by New English Library

British Library C.I.P.

Satchell, Tim
Royal romance: Prince Andrew and
Sarah Ferguson.
1. Andrew, *Prince, son of Elizabeth II,*
Queen of Great Britain   2. Ferguson, Sarah
3. Great Britain – Princes and princesses
– Biography
I. Title
941.085′092′2   DA591.A1

ISBN 0-450-40247-9

Printed and bound in Great Britain for
Hodder and Stoughton Paperbacks, a
division of Hodder and Stoughton Ltd.,
Mill Road, Dunton Green, Sevenoaks,
Kent (Editorial Office: 47 Bedford
Square, London WC1B 3DP) by
Richard Clay (The Chaucer Press) Ltd.,
Bungay, Suffolk. Photoset by
Rowland Phototypesetting Ltd.,
Bury St Edmunds, Suffolk.

Acknowledgement

To the 137 people who
helped – many thanks

Contents

Photographs

Royal Romance
Prince Andrew
and
Sarah Ferguson

Prologue

Her left hand entwined in Andrews right, Fergie drew a short breath as the Archbishop, resplendent in his mitre and white, purple and gold vestments, began:
'I, SARAH MARGARET,'
  She paused a fraction and repeated, clearly: 'I, SARAH MARGARET.'

'Take thee, ANDREW ALBERT CHRISTIAN ED-WARD,'
'Take thee, ANDREW ALBERT CHRISTIAN,' – she stumbled and continued, 'CHRISTIAN ED-WARD,'

'To my wedded husband,'
'To my wedded husband,'

'To have and to hold,'
'To have and to hold,'

'From this day forward,'
'From this day forward,'

'For better for worse,'
'For better for worse,'

'For richer for poorer,'
'For richer for poorer,'

'*In sickness and in health,*'
'In sickness and in health,'

'*To love, cherish,*'
'To love, cherish,'

'*And to obey,*'

Fergie looked at Andrew, and she tightened her grip on his hand slightly. 'And to obey,'

'*Till death us do part,*'
'Till death us do part,'

'*According to God's holy ordinance;*'
'According to God's holy ordinance;'

'*And thereto I give thee my troth.*'
'And thereto I give thee my troth.'

The Archbishop continued alone: 'In thy name, O Lord, we hallow and dedicate this ring, that by thy blessing he who gives it and she who wears it, keeping true faith the one to the other, may abide together in thy peace, continue together in thy favour, live together in thy love, and may finally dwell together in thine eternal kingdom; through Jesus Christ our Lord. *Amen.*'

Prince Edward had placed not one, but two rings on the service book in the clergyman's hands. First Andrew took one ring of Welsh gold and placed it on the fourth finger of Sarah's left hand. Then Sarah, with just a shade of difficulty, and not for the first time, helped out by Andrew, placed a fine band of gold next to the signet ring that Andrew wears on the little finger of his left hand.

She could feel her hand shaking, ever so slightly, and a thought went through her mind: whatever happened she didn't want to let him down by fainting. But he held her hand and followed the Archbishop in saying the vows for both of them:

'With this ring, I thee wed, with my body, I thee worship, and with all my worldly goods I thee endow: In the name of the Father, and of the Son, and of the Holy Ghost. *Amen*.'

Fergie, Princess Andrew, the Duchess of York dared to look at him once again. Their eyes met. There may have been grey clouds, trials, tribulations and problems for both of them, but this, they knew, was a perfect moment.

It was later, at Buckingham Palace, that Sarah let out a big sigh. At the lunch, as the guests toasted her in Bollinger champagne, to an enquiry from a close friend, Fergie said, '*That* was wonderful. But, boy, am I glad that *that's* over.'

Royal Romance
Prince Andrew
and
Sarah Ferguson

1

A Good Team

This is not a fairy-tale romance of a rather plain, ordinary little girl who grew into a beautiful princess. Rather it is the story of a rather plain, ordinary and friendly little girl who grew into a rather plain, ordinary and friendly big girl and then, to the amazement of many and the delight of all, blossomed overnight into a glamorous princess.

As one old friend says, not unkindly: 'Lively, dumpy, Fergie. Who would have believed it? Every girl should have a best friend like her, and so should every man.'

When His Royal Highness Prince Andrew Albert Christian Edward chose as his bride a vivacious, freckle-faced redhead called Sarah Ferguson both their lives were inexorably changed. For him there lies a new, mature role and new responsibilities. For her there is a daunting and difficult future, almost impossible to imagine.

Gone are the easy-going days of the bachelor girl. Gone is the informality of life in a South London flat. Gone are the problems of saving up for a new outfit and counting the pennies until the next payday. Home is now a palace, uniformed guardsmen at the gate. Her every wish is a command. An outing is now a state occasion or a banquet for visiting heads of government. And every move she makes will be examined, reported and often distorted. She will need all her reserves of good humour, vitality and stamina. But she has already shown that she will manage and manage well. And already she has been taken to the nation's heart.

She is not a natural beauty, but is all the better for that as the beauty she does have comes from within. She is cheerful, positive, home-loving, and will happily adapt to whatever Andrew requires from a wife. Perhaps Sarah's greatest asset is that she is unfazeable. Whatever happens, she will cope. This is an essential quality for a princess, and will make life easier in the early days when, for instance, if she buys new clothes she will be accused of extravagance, if she doesn't, of dowdiness. If she outshines the Princess of Wales she will be an upstart, and she will equally be told to seek Diana's advice if she doesn't.

That unfazeability has been gained in a hard school: as a teenager when her mother left home to live with another man; when there were other women around her father; when he remarried; when her greatest friend, her sister, left to live on the other side of the world; when her father started a new family; and finally when she had the experience of a free-living lover far older than herself.

As for Prince Andrew, he has followed in the footsteps of his elder brother and sister by marrying a British-born commoner. Traditionally the royal families of Europe have intermarried, originally for the sake of political expediency and international alliance, and latterly, out of sheer snobbishness, but this generation of the royal family have consistently chosen for themselves.

In Sarah, Andrew has found a girl who will be welcomed into his family and, as importantly, will be welcomed by the vast majority of British people who regard the royal family as their own. They are, in Sarah's own words, 'a good team'.

For neither is it their first grand passion, and friends of the couple feel that they are not blindly in love but that the marriage is a carefully considered decision. They certainly like each other a lot, enjoy each other's company and from that strong base a great love can grow.

As always with the royal family, a lot of nonsense has been talked about Andrew and Sarah. So let us begin by looking at some of the facts:

Prince Andrew is called Andrew by the Queen and Prince Philip – in his turn, he refers to them as Mother and Father in private and as the Queen and Prince Philip or, just occasionally, 'My father' in the presence of others. Prince Charles, Princess Diana and Princess Anne also call him Andrew. In the Navy most officers call him H (for Highness – his full rank is Lieutenant His Royal Highness the Prince Andrew). A few of his more intimate officer friends in the Navy call him Andrew, very occasionally abbreviated to Andy, or else Frog (as in 'kiss a frog and get a prince'). The ratings invariably refer to him – behind his back, at least – as Andy.

Sarah Ferguson is known to her close friends, friends and contemporaries as Fergie. Prince Andrew calls her Fergie, or Fergs. She calls him Andrew or Darling. She signs herself Fergie to friends and Sarah Ferguson to acquaintances and business contacts; it is always Fergie with an 'ie', and never Fergy with a 'y'.

Unlike Charles and Diana, who are never, but never, referred to as Chuck and Di, Andrew and Sarah really are referred to as Andy and Fergie, although Andrew does prefer his name to be spelt out in full.

Andrew is a straightforward, fairly decent fellow. Yet for all that he has seen and done, he is surprisingly naïve and unworldly in some ways. It is a rather endearing trait, almost as though, on occasions, he assumes that if he can't see the world, the world can't see him – an ostrich, head-in-the-sand view. He is quite different in personality from his brother Charles, whom he greatly admires and looks up to. While Charles has a subtle and mellow approach to life, and will always examine all sides of a situation, Andrew has a robust humour, often unrestrained by what he might consider to be petty sensibilities. But then he, like all the royal family, has led a remarkably sheltered and protected life, even though they are now in the public eye more than ever before. In the past he has fallen in love easily and when he falls, he falls hard.

He was concerned that his life would be spent as a

ribbon-cutting and ship-launching automaton, but after initial doubts about his twelve-year naval commission, he now feels that he has found a vocation. He would like to carry on his life in relative peace, taking advantage of his action-filled time in the Navy with the on-shore life of the wealthy young man he is.

If there is no traditional fairy-tale heroine in this story, then there is a fairy-tale character who plays a large part. For, whatever Fergie's father may say, the main figure in the background is Princess Diana. Just as the match between Charles and Diana was a major triumph for the Queen Mother and Ruth, Lady Fermoy, the respective maternal grandmothers, so, for Diana, the marriage of Andrew and Fergie is a major coup. Diana didn't make the match; that is done elsewhere. But if marriages are made in Heaven, on earth they invariably have a geographical location. And Andrew and Fergie's match was made possible by Diana, firstly at Kensington Palace and then at Sandringham.

When Diana Spencer married Prince Charles she was an unformed, but willing, character and the occasional unfortunate clashes with those who surrounded her were, and are, not surprising. There are unlikely to be any such clashes with Fergie, as she already knows how to deal with people. It was essential that Prince Charles, as the future King, should marry a girl of integrity, discretion and purity. Or maybe those qualities should be listed in reverse order. Now that Charles has two healthy sons, the obligation to marry a virgin bride was not placed on Andrew. Indeed the fear was that Andrew, with his liking for the more flighty, glamorous-looking girls – albeit rather nice ones – might end up demanding to marry some showbusiness flibberti-gibbet.

The engagement was short and so, relatively, was the courtship. But as Andrew says: 'We wanted to get on with it.' And almost everyone who has lived through a lengthy engagement and prenuptial romance knows that the time leading up to the wedding is by far the most difficult for the relationship – and imagine how much more difficult with the world's press on one's doorstep.

Why are the press there? Well, with no disrespect, the British royal family – the Family Firm, as the Queen calls it – is the longest-running and most successful soap opera in the world. All the ingredients are there: power, money, splendour, tradition, adventure, religion, sex and romance, hopes, dreams, even occasional disappointments. Like any successful soap opera the ratings, which are already sky-high, are always boosted by some new twist to the story, or the appearance of some new character on the stage.

There are a number of reasons for the marriage, which will emerge during the course of this book. But there are two main ones: Fergie and Andrew are in love, and Fergie is the first of Andrew's real girlfriends who was acceptable to Buckingham Palace. He wanted to marry Koo Stark, but she was American, four years older than him, and an actress – worse, she was alleged to have appeared in pornographic movies. This allegation was grossly unfair – like many other young actresses she accepted roles in a couple of rather poor movies in which she appeared naked. These were scarcely more pornographic than a newspaper pin-up, but Koo paid a terrible price for them. But she was Andrew's first true love and he still sees Koo and frequently talks to her on the telephone.

Fergie, as some are keen to tell us, has had two lovers in her twenty-six years. Discounting the fact that this is somewhat fewer than Andrew has had, they were long-term, serious relationships and, fun-loving though she is, she was never one to fool around and always stayed faithful to her man.

While Prince Charles's genuine, if awkward, search for knowledge has been mocked, Andrew's sometimes poor behaviour has more often been described as youthful high spirits. Charles, who has always been aware of the strictures that rule his life, was genuinely envious of Andrew's involvement in the Falklands war. While he has resigned himself to twinges of envy for the freedom that Andrew has enjoyed with his romantic life, he is rather looking forward to being on an equal footing with him again. After Andrew's rompings in the West Indies and his spraying of paint on watching newsmen, it was left to the small-circulation *Spectator* to draw comparison between Andrew and Prime Minister Margaret Thatcher's son Mark: 'common young men . . . a disgrace to their parents'. Now Fergie is expected to give Andrew new maturity.

By marrying into the royal family, Fergie is also becoming a supernumerary member of the court. The court, official and unofficial, that surrounds the Queen is large and very influential. Its proceedings, manoeuvres and activities are rarely accurately described, and hardly ever penetrated. Yet the court, which includes politicians, members of the armed services, royal staff, some peers and the Queen's circle of confidants, makes the most important decisions in the country. In its own way the court is far more powerful than Parliament and the Queen herself. It is the court that decides what is right, correct, and what can and can not be done by the royal family. The court has already welcomed Fergie to its inner sanctum and has given its blessing to the marriage. The court too determines the role that will be played by the new royal couple, based on Andrew's position in the line of succession to the throne. This is at present as follows:

1 Prince Charles
2 Prince William
3 Prince Henry
4 Prince Andrew
5 Prince Edward

Any children of Prince Andrew would come before Prince Edward; equally, any further children of Prince Charles would come before Prince Andrew. Fergie, as a newcomer to the royal family, does not feature in the list of succession although, at present, she would become Queen in the event of the death or abdication of the Queen, Prince Charles, Prince William and Prince Henry – a not entirely unfeasible scenario given their informal exposure, Charles's enjoyment of travelling with his family, and the present climate of international terrorism.

And Fergie is herself distantly related to the royal family. She is a descendant of Charles II, through an illegitimate line of his mistress Lucy Walters, and has some twenty-five lines of descent from Henry VII. Andrew and Fergie are sixth cousins, once removed, through both the 2nd Duke of Portland and the 4th Duke of Devonshire. Through the 1st Duke of Abercorn, every one of whose six daughters married a duke, a marquess or an earl, Fergie is a fourth cousin of Princess Diana – the late and eccentric Irish peer, the Earl of Wicklow (Evelyn Waugh's Oxford friend 'Cracky' Clonmore) claimed that the Abercorns had a black ancestor whose blood would one day resurface. By marriage she is distantly related to Peter Ustinov. Among her direct forebears are the 1st Duke of Marlborough and Samuel Whitbread, brewer and MP who, according to an early *Burke*'s *Landed Gentry*, 'in a paroxysm of mental aberration terminated his existence'.

So as far as the court and the rest of the world are concerned, Sarah Ferguson's official title is now Her Royal Highness the Princess Andrew. But she still likes her friends to call her Fergie.

2

The Ferguson Family

Ronald Ivor Ferguson was born in 1931, the second son of Major (later Colonel) Andrew Ferguson, known to his friends as Fergie. The death from peritonitis of Ronald's brother John Andrew, two and half years older, just one month after his tenth birthday, had little effect on the younger boy. While Ronald had always been the grubby one, the troublemaker, John was always well-behaved and the brothers were not close. But from then on Ronald was raised as an only child – having been number two in line he was suddenly the one on whom his father pinned his hopes.

Ronald followed his father to Eton and into the Life Guards – his father had become Commanding Officer when he was nine. In time Ronald rose to the rank of Major and became Commander of the Sovereign's Escort of the Household Cavalry. But as a six-foot-plus, dashing and handsome young Lieutenant he fell for Susie Wright, a sparkling blonde and the youngest of the four children of Doreen – grandchild of Irish peer Lord Powerscroft (pronounced Paws-court) – and FitzHerbert Wright, formerly 15th/19th Hussars, director of the engineering Coal and Iron Company. The Wrights lived at Bridgewater House in Grantham, Lincolnshire – incidentally, the birthplace of Margaret Thatcher.

Susie's mother Doreen (née Wingfield) and Ronald's mother Marian (née Montagu-Douglas-Scott) were old friends, and Mrs Doreen Wright says: 'I really don't know exactly when they met, they've known each other since childhood. We lived in Lincolnshire then, so it could have been out hunting with the Belvoir' (pronounced Beaver, and one of the smart hunts in the area with whom, in more recent times, Prince Charles has ridden).

The Ferguson family is of once prosperous Irish stock, and the Wrights are still thriving. Susie's three sisters married well: in 1950 Brigid, nine years older, married Julian Salmond, son of Marshal of the RAF Sir John Salmond; Davina, six years older, married baronet Sir Richard Boughey the same year; her brother Bryan, three years older, has never married and, after Eton and twenty years in the Blues and Royals cavalry regiment and some time travelling in Africa and gambling, he is now happily employed as a butler to the Duke of Devonshire's cousin Hugh Cavendish at Holker Hall in Cumbria.

Ronald Ferguson was also well-connected, being a cousin of the Duke of Buccleuch, and when he asked Susie to marry him, she accepted with alacrity despite her youth. They were from similar backgrounds and had friends and interests in common. It seemed, at the time, a good match. He was twenty-four and she was eighteen when they walked down the aisle of St Margaret's, Westminster, in the shadow of Westminster Abbey. Friends from those days say she was one of the great beauties of her age, in both looks and spirit, and that she made a ravishing bride as she walked with her handsome husband under the bridal arch of Life Guards' ceremonial swords.

They moved to Lowood House, in Sunninghill, Berkshire, and just one year later – Ronald now a captain – on Monday, 26 August 1957, their first child, Jane Louisa, was born at the Welbeck Nursing Home, 27 Welbeck Street, London. Within another two years, early on the morning of Thursday, 15 October 1959, their second daughter, Sarah Margaret, was born with a little tuft of fair ginger hair on her head. Like Jane, Sarah was given names that had been in the family for years, and was not named for any person in particular.

Ronald Ferguson had started playing polo when he was with the Life Guards in the Canal Zone in 1954 and the game soon became a major obsession in his life. It had speed, horsemanship, sportsmanship and camaraderie. So when he came to Smith's Lawn in 1955, as a subaltern protégé of Lord Mountbatten who had befriended him, he started playing in earnest. One of the first friends he made on the polo field was Prince Philip.

It was the Persians in 600 BC who first played polo – the hockey on horseback that takes its name from the Tibetan Kasmiri-dialect Balti word 'polo' for 'ball'. It spread east, and had all but died out by the nineteenth century when British officers in India rediscovered it, collected the rules and developed the game we know today, with four-a-side mounted players wielding long sticks with mallet heads to hit the solid wooden ball. A game, which will wear out several polo balls, consists of between four and six seven-minute periods, known as chukkas from the Hindi 'cakkar' for 'round', after each of which the small, tough, agile ponies are changed. It is a fast and furious game and very much, whatever anyone may say, a rich man's sport. Despite its enthusiastic following in England, the sport has been dominated by Argentina: for players, ponies and grooms.

Like any other rich man's sport there are cheaper ways of playing, but a serious player would need at least half-a-dozen ponies each costing anything up to £10,000 or more, approximately £50 a week to keep, and around £80 a week for one or more grooms to care for them. For the rich – and there is no one in this country wealthier than the royal family – there are three polo centres: at Cirencester Park, Cowdray Park, and the Guards Polo Club at Smith's Lawn in Windsor.

Smith's Lawn is in the middle of Windsor Great Park, with beautifully tended grounds and facilities in the middle of the oak woods and a rhododendron plantation close to Windsor Castle. The rent-free grounds are owned by the Queen, but run entirely by the Club, and that is where Prince Philip, who had been introduced to the game by his uncle, Earl Mountbatten of Burma, author (as the pseudonymous Marco) of the definitive *An Introduction to*

Polo, liked to play. And it was here that he became on intimate terms with Major Ronald Ferguson. It was also at Smith's Lawn that Prince Charles learnt to play polo and discovered his enthusiasm for the game.

Of course, that was before Prince Philip developed the synoritis that made him take up horse-and-carriage driving instead. Now Prince Philip's problems have worsened and he has had to concentrate on his carriage-driving activities, and the carriage-driving centre he has started at Sandringham, but in Major Ferguson's daughter he has regained his links with his polo-playing days.

It was not surprising that Prince Philip and Ronald Ferguson were drawn to each other. The indispensable aide to the Duke of Windsor, as Prince of Wales, was Major Edward 'Fruity' Metcalfe, who managed the Prince's polo ponies and was later best man at his wedding to Wallis Simpson. Prince Philip had become a founder member of the Guards Polo Club at Windsor Great Park in 1952, when the site of the last Prince of Wales's airstrip was turned into Smith's Lawn.

Major Ferguson, a first cousin of Princess Alice, Duchess of Gloucester, was the nephew of Jane, wife of William Fellowes (made Sir William in 1964), the Queen's much-respected land agent at Sandringham and previously, from 1936 to 1952, land agent to her father.

Over the years, a definite friendship between Prince Philip and the Queen and the Fergusons developed, so that they were invited to Sandringham and Buckingham Palace. They had their polo in common and they enjoyed each other's company. Indeed, there is a perfectly true story concerning a Trooping of the Colour ceremony when Major Ferguson, the immaculate Commander of the Queen's Escort, riding alongside Her Majesty, edged slightly ahead. The Queen, out of the side of her mouth, good-humouredly spoke to Ferguson, saying: 'Back a bit, Ron. They've come to see me, not you.'

On the polo field Prince Philip and Ronald Ferguson, along with John Lucas, were the joint best English players with a five-goal handicap, and off the field Prince Philip was very taken with Ronald's lively wife, Susie: they would laugh together, chat together and frankly the Queen was quite happy for him to have found a dance partner – if she took the dance floor with Philip people would sometimes stand back and look awkward, there wasn't that problem when Philip danced with Susie.

One newspaper even spent some time unsuccessfully trying to prove a romance between Prince Philip and Susie Ferguson. There was no doubt though that Susie, who had married so very young and who had grown apart from her husband with his laconic Anglo-Saxon attitude, greatly enjoyed the attention that Philip paid her, particularly since her husband found irresistible the company of the many attractive girls around, whether grooms or camp-followers.

Despite Ferguson's admiration of pretty girls, he has always held an ambivalent view of social life. He does not drink and he does not like crowds, yet his life and work is essentially social and he has always enjoyed his courtier-dom. He says: 'I hate the social whirl absolutely. I'm never happier than when I'm just sitting in my pyjamas and dressing-gown at home. I hate being social, can't stand cock-tail parties. One has to go to a lot of things but I can't wait to get to my car and get away and drive down back home.

'I'm almost completely teetotal. I might possibly have one glass of wine at a dinner party or a ball or dance. It's because my mother and father didn't drink and I don't like alcohol.'

It is impossible to say exactly when Sarah and Andrew met, as she would come up to the Guards Polo Club with her mother and sister to see her father playing polo, as did Prince Andrew with his mother. But as far as can be established they must have been three or four years old on that first fateful occasion.

The Fergusons lived at Lowood House in Sunninghill until the death of Ronald's father Andrew in 1966, when it was decided that the family would move to Dummer Down

House and take over the running of the farm. Ronald,
having met with no great success at Staff College, decided
in 1967 that he would leave the Army after he had completed nineteen years at the end of the following year. His
ponies came with him from Ribblesdale Park, near the polo
club, where he had been ticked off – and questions were
asked by MPs – when he had too conspicuously deployed
one of his men to duties looking after them. 'Being found
out like that is spoiling it for the rest of us,' grumbled a
fellow officer. At Dummer Down Farm, a mixed arable
farm which currently employs six, with a foreman and a
herdsman for the milking herd of Fresians, Ferguson had
plenty of space and stabling.

Leaving Lowood House and leaving the Army was an
upheaval in many ways. Within two years Ronald's mother
married Air Marshal Sir Thomas Elmhirst, a former
Lieutenant Governor of Guernsey, eleven years older than
her and who had been widowed three years earlier, and they
moved into The Cottage in the village of Dummer itself.

The M3 motorway to Southampton from London has
only ever gone as far as Exit 7 – and at Exit 7 there is a
notice saying 'Dummer Only'; it goes nowhere else. Popular local gossip, not surprisingly denied by the authorities,
is that this is expressly so that Major Ferguson can reach
Windsor with ease and so that Prince Philip could go to
consult the major and examine any ponies. It is a forty-
minute drive to Windsor Great Park in Ferguson's dark
orange BMW 320 with its mascot in the likeness of a
late-lamented Jack Russell called Mr Bugs. His office is in a
simple long wooden hut and he does have, as he describes
it, the perfect job. 'I've been terribly lucky,' he says.

Polo must seem an extraordinary sport to many. In
England there are no big prizes, just the joys of winning.
The playing season runs from May to the beginning of
September, with different levels of play: high goal, medium
goal and low goal. In the low-goal games the handicaps
must not add up to more than 6 (sometimes 8) and there are
4 chukkas; in medium-goal games the handicap total is 15;

and in the high-goal games, the most exciting, the handicaps must not add up to more than 22. 10 is the best handicap, and -2 is the lowest. Usually there are two professionals – in former days invariably Argentinian, playing off between 6 and 9 goals – the wealthy patron, who will often be the worst player, and one other.

For the Les Diables Bleus team run by Guy Wildenstein, son of international art dealer and racehorse owner Daniel Wildenstein, Prince Charles, a useful player with a 4 handicap, was 'the other'. There are worse ways of entering the polo world's inner circle than being rich, buying a large string of top animals, hiring a couple of world-class professionals and inviting one of the polo establishment, such as Major Ferguson, to play for the team.

A knowledge of the sport is essential to understand the position of the professionals. They invariably come from a wealthy and privileged background. The Argentinians in particular breed, break, train and sell the ponies to supplement the salaries – upwards of £10,000 a season – they would be paid by their patrons. They live in accommodation provided by their patrons and deal with them on equal terms for the season which starts with Queen's Cup at Windsor in May and continues with the Warwick Cup at Cirencester and goes on to the greatest of all polo prizes, the Gold Cup at Cowdray Park. Then after the season in England they winter in Florida, where there are large prizes to be played for and plenty of super-wealthy patrons – although the aficionados say that the polo is not in the same class as the English game.

One of the finest teams seen in Britain in recent years was that of Stowell Park, run by Sam Vestey – Lord Vestey – a millionaire many times over from his meat interests in South America, and his brother Mark, now tragically crippled after a hunting accident. The two professionals in the Vestey team, named after the magnificent Vestey home in Gloucestershire, were among the finest in the land, Eduardo Moore and Hector Barrantes. The latter was an athletic and swarthy six-footer who had arrived in England in 1967 at the age of twenty-eight, not speaking a word of English.

Behind Ronald Ferguson's military bearing, insistence on correct procedure and occasional sharpness of speech which sometimes make him seem pompous and aloof, there is a warm-hearted and kind man, excellent with horses, but not quite so good with his fellow man. He was always good with Sarah and Jane, although at some distance. He has done a tremendous amount for polo – 'What I'd like to do is to get it out of the gossip columns and on to the sports pages,' he says – and as a promotions man he is superb.

His first wife Susie is quite a different character. She is naturally outgoing, sparkling, friendly and emotional. When Jane and Sarah were small she suffered from the loss of the third child she had been expecting – she was told afterwards that she would be unable to have any more and she had a hysterectomy – and the growing gulf between herself and her husband. She would sometimes go to London and stay at their house in First Street, Chelsea, while he was happy to spend his time at home in the country with his animals.

Despite his country interests, Ronald Ferguson is not a huntin', shootin', fishin' type, as his image may suggest. He doesn't hunt, says that he is delighted to get off a horse at the end of the polo season and, anyway, he thinks the hunting around Hampshire would be an anti-climax after the hunting of his youth in Warwickshire. He has never fished and some fifteen years ago he decided to give up shooting. As he explains: 'I considered that I no longer had the right to take a bird's life. I haven't shot since.'

Ferguson's work at the Guards Polo Club (first as Liaison Officer, now as Deputy Chairman) and closeness to the royal family also meant that, as Prince Charles's involvement and enthusiasm for polo grew, in 1971 Ferguson became the unofficial polo manager to the prince, teaching, encouraging, finding horses and fixing matches. There is no fee paid and Ferguson is not on any official list, yet the job became increasingly important. Now the prince's horses are looked after at Windsor Castle by Charles's groom Raoul, known as Charlie's Argie, but if there are new animals to be tried or breeding to be organised, it is Ronald Ferguson who does it. This role is so major that he is referred to behind his back – but with his knowledge – as 'Polo-stick in Waiting'.

The Vesteys' popular Stowell Park player Hector Barrantes suffered an appalling tragedy when his Argentinian wife, Louisa James, eight months pregnant after fourteen years of marriage, was killed in a car crash. Hector's right leg was badly fractured (he wears a copper bangle to ward off rheumatism even now) and his sister, who was driving them on the Buenos Aires road, escaped major injury. Barrantes was heartbroken, and the tragedy was the cause of much concern among his friends on and off the polo field in England.

Ronald and Susie Ferguson suggested that, at the end of the season, Barrantes should join them and some friends – Fred Winter's daughter Philippa was among the mixed party – at the villa where they were planning to holiday in Corfu. It was a fateful invitation.

For by the end of that holiday, in an atmosphere of wine, food and sun, Susie, who had little experience of life before she married, was hopelessly smitten by the macho Barrantes, who was everything that her husband was not. And Barrantes was totally charmed and captivated by the lively Susie.

Among their close friends it did not come as a great surprise when Susie Ferguson decided that there was no future in her marriage to Ferguson. Ronald Ferguson claimed to understand her views, but thought they should continue. Just think of the shame . . . their friends . . . their girls. He believed that the children were the strength that would keep the family together. But he had reckoned without the strength of purpose that he had so much admired in Susie when they were younger. As far as Susie was concerned, the marriage was over and she was not going to lose the opportunity of true happiness with Hector Barrantes, who, as well as being a first-class polo player, was good-looking, charming, kind, attentive and understanding. Barrantes, two years younger than Susie, was known by some on the polo circuit as The Godfather for the manipulative energy with which he was sometimes credited, but this was not the image he wanted to create at all. He is also, according to one of Britain's top players, 'a real gentleman, and a delightful man and a brilliant polo player. You could not hope to meet a nicer person.'

Barrantes did not break up the marriage; to all intents and purposes it was over already. But Susie was blindly in love for the first time in her life. While she was not always sure she was doing the right thing, the situation was far worse for Barrantes. For he was a mainstay of the Vestey team in England and a colleague of Peter Brant in the United States, and he depended on their patronage. He was concerned that to go off with another man's wife – and, worse, the wife of such a key figure in the polo establishment – would be professional suicide. Indeed, for a time he did seem to be backing away from the relationship and had serious doubts about continuing it, but eventually Susie left her husband to move in with him. She had done nothing like this before and had had no lovers when she was younger, but now, for her, it was time to make the break.

Ferguson was devastated. Fergie told friends: 'It is the only time that I have ever seen my father cry.' But some friends of the couple believe he was less devastated by losing Susie than by the grubby business – in those days – of going through the divorce courts, the perceived humiliation made worse by the fact that the man she had run off with was not an English gentleman but a Latin.

Susie agreed to let him have whatever he wanted – she could have demanded a share in the farm, at least, and possibly custody of the children. But the Fergusons did agree that least harm would be done by trying to remain on amicable terms and so Susie would go but the children would stay. In true military style, Ferguson gritted his teeth and decided there was no alternative but to carry on. The children were looked after by a housekeeper so there was little change to his lifestyle, except that when he went out to dinner he was now a divorced man and needed a female partner.

Susie moved in with Hector at Little Bromshole, in the small Sussex village of Iping, just outside Midhurst. The Ferguson marriage was dissolved in 1974: Susie agreed to give Ronald custody of the children, although she would have the normal access rights. She had a small private income of her own, and settled for the proceeds of the small house in Chelsea to which she had contributed and took with her some of the family jewels.

'Of course the divorce was a trauma for the girls,' says Ferguson, 'particularly at that vulnerable age. It was a bit of a fright, to put it mildly, for everybody. It meant that at that age the children didn't have a mother, she had disappeared.'

But if events devastated Major Ferguson, their effect on his two teenage daughters was inestimable. It might have seemed that the lives of the girls, as weekly boarders were not too disrupted. And it was a convenient scheme for Ferguson and Susie. The English public-school system means that full boarders are only at home for four weeks at Christmas, four weeks at Easter and maybe eight weeks in the summer; weekly boarders might see their homes more, but they are still based away from their home for much of the year.

Both girls became withdrawn and quiet. They didn't talk to their schoolfriends about it as there was little that they could do to help. Jane, at fifteen, was deeply self-conscious and her situation was made worse by the fact that she had no mother at home to run to when needed. The Fergusons weren't the only children of split families, but there was little comfort in this. Susie did see them often and they went to stay with her in the holidays, but it would be foolish to pretend that the relationship could ever be the same.

Sarah, aged thirteen, after an initial outburst or two,

appeared less affected by the separation. Eventually the atmosphere at home with her father improved, and she would go with Jane and their mother to see Hector play polo – Jane would stay quietly in the background, while Fergie rushed around. The girls compensated for their loss of a mother in those difficult early teens by becoming even closer than they were previously, although the external signs of their insecurity were opposite, with Jane becoming increasingly solemn and thoughtful and Fergie more and more outgoing. One groom who used to work for Prince Charles recalls: 'I remember Sarah's curly red hair was always around the place. She was hugely energetic. She was like a bubble that was about to burst.'

The biggest problem for Jane and Sarah was caused by their divided loyalty to their parents, Sarah seemed able to cope with this, coming through the separation and divorce with a surface dignity that belied her years. Jane had a rougher ride. But underneath, and over the longer-term, it hurt Sarah and left a yawning gap in her growing-up. She never spoke to her friends about the divorce, even to those to whom she was closest and who had been through the same thing; instead she quietly nursed her feelings to herself. The final break in the old life came on 25 July 1975 when Susie and Hector married at Chichester Register Office with two polo-player witnesses, Juan MacDonough and Gonzales Pieres. Some reports have suggested that Major Ferguson and Hector Barrantes did not meet after Susie left. But that is not so. The divorce was as amicable as these things can be and the polo world is so small that they couldn't help but meet, and meet frequently.

Some of their friends went one way, some the other. But one of the most surprising things about the divorce and remarriage, and one which shows the esteem in which Prince Philip held Susie, was the speed with which they were accepted back into the polo and the royal circle.

The business of looking after two young girls was one that Ferguson tackled in a coolly logical way. 'Father took over and did his best, but it doesn't matter what the father takes upon himself or what he does, there is no substitute for a mother at that age. None whatsoever. They were weekly boarders. At weekends I could keep them busy with riding horses and things,' he says. He claims not to have been an over-indulgent father. 'I thought it would be a ghastly mistake to try and compensate financially, with things or with kindness and that kind of thing. That would have had the worst effect later on. I knew whatever I did had to stand them in good stead for the future, on their own two feet. I tried desperately hard not to spoil them and I think I succeeded.'

3

Gordonstoun and Girls

Prince Philip once made the memorable remark that 'People want their first child very much. They want the second almost as much. If a third comes along, they accept it as natural, but they haven't gone out of their way to try and get it.'

Prince Andrew came along, to use Philip's expression, at Buckingham Palace in the early afternoon of Friday, 19 February 1960, the first child to be born to a reigning monarch for over a hundred years, since Queen Victoria gave birth to her daughter Princess Beatrice, later Princess Henry of Battenberg, in 1857.

His Royal Highness Prince Andrew Albert Christian Edward was the third child, and second son, of Queen Elizabeth II and the Duke of Edinburgh. He was the first of the Queen's second batch of children, with Prince Charles (born 14 November 1948) and Princess Anne (born 15 August 1950) twelve and ten years older and, finally, Prince Edward, born Prince Edward Antony Richard Louis, arriving four years later on Tuesday, 10 March 1964. Prince Philip's comments on fourth children are not available.

Thanks to the British rule of primogeniture, whereby the eldest son gets everything, Prince Charles, at his mother's succession in 1952, gained an impressive array of titles: Prince of Wales, Earl of Chester, Duke of Cornwall and Rothesay, Earl of Carrick and Baron of Renfrew, Lord of the Isle and Great Steward of Scotland. Prince Andrew gained nothing, except his position as second in line to the throne. At one time that position, to all intents and purposes, would have carried little significance – but that was before the traumatic events that led to Andrew's grandfather becoming King in 1936.

The Duke of York, second son of King George V, had been brought up to remain in the shadow of his brother David, Prince of Wales. It was always known that David would be treated and trained for kingship, while Prince George would ever remain the second string, standing in when absolutely necessary, living the life of peripheral royalty but hardly worth the expenditure of any great effort. That was reckoning without the character of the putative king, fawned to from an early age. Far from being a strong and kingly person, David developed into a rather weak character, with a love of all things foppish, all things American and all things with a veneer of glamour.

Nevertheless he was adored by the people in the country during those lean and difficult 1930s. The trends he set were many and various. When he wore plus-fours the world followed. The Prince of Wales' check was named after a particularly loud pattern he favoured. When the prince smoked, the world smoked. When the prince patronised the American dancers Fred and Adèle Astaire, so did the world. So, when divorcée Mrs Wallis Warfield Simpson set her cap at him, the prince was smitten and could only imagine that the world would follow him in thinking that he could marry her. Finally, faced with rejection of his wilfulness, he did the unthinkable and abdicated in 1936 having reigned for just 325 days, uncrowned, as Edward VII. It was the first time in England's history that a king had abdicated since pre-Norman Conquest times, when King Ethelwulf was deposed while travelling in Europe with his youngest son Alfred (later the Great) by his eldest son Ethelbald in 856 and decided to abdicate rather than start a civil war.

Some say that Wallis Simpson enjoyed being a friend and confidante of the prince, was quite happy with that status and was taken aback by the king's ardour and abdication: that she had no choice but to marry him, having strung him along. Whatever the facts, the situation left George VI unprepared for his new role and the monarchy went through a particularly shaky period. Since then the impossible has always been considered and Andrew was brought up and educated so that he, too, could be king.

Maybe the precautions are unnecessary. For a long time there have been rumblings among some of the more left-wing politicians about abolishing the House of Lords, and if that ever happened it would be considerably easier to abolish the monarchy as well. But certainly, twice this century, with George V and George VI, second sons have succeeded to the throne.

Following royal tradition, Andrew was christened in the Music Room at Buckingham Palace wearing the robe of Honiton lace designed for the baptism of Queen Victoria's children. He was named after Prince Philip's father, Prince Andrew of Greece, and St Andrew of Scotland, the first member of the British royal family to be named Andrew for over five hundred years. Using water from the font brought from Windsor especially for the occasion, the Archbishop of Canterbury also named him Albert, after the Queen's father who reigned as King George but was always affectionately known as Bertie, and Queen Victoria's consort (she had said that she wanted all her descendants to bear his name). Christian and Edward were from his great-grandparents, Christian IX of Denmark and Edward VII.

Andrew was also the first Mountbatten-Windsor, the Queen decreeing that although she and her children would be known as the House and Family of Windsor, their descendants would bear the name Mountbatten-Windsor in deference to Prince Philip.

The Queen did her best in those early days to shield Andrew from the outside world. By now experienced in her duties, she had more time and attention to lavish on him as a child than she had with Charles and Anne. He started his education under a governess at Buckingham Palace with a couple of playmates, mixing with 'outsiders' in the weekly meetings of the First Marylebone Cub Scouts in the grounds of Buckingham Palace. Andrew, a boisterous youngster, would always be in the forefront of any fun.

As a child his untrammelled 'high spirits', as the nannies optimistically called them, involved such pranks as driving his pedal-car full tilt at the royal dorgis – those strange animals created by the mating of the Queen's corgi bitch with Princess Margaret's dachsund dog. Or else having rumbustious fights, 'beating up' the indulgent Charles on the Palace lawns.

One of the benefits of being a member of the royal family is to take advantage of the gifts that pour into the Palace, most of which are given away – there was a whole warehouse full of teddybears when Diana gave birth to Prince William, every one of which went to charities and hospitals. So, at the age of seven, Andrew had graduated to a scale working-model Aston Martin – given as a publicity gimmick by the James Bond film-makers. This was one present that was not given away, and Andrew became a regular menace as he whizzed around the gardens – the car had a top speed of about five miles an hour. Otherwise his energies were directed to learning such tricks as tying together the shoelaces of the stone-faced guards on duty at the Palace.

He didn't follow Charles to Cheam School, the preparatory school in Surrey where his brother (the first prince to be educated away from the Palace) and father had gone, as Charles had not enjoyed it. It was thought that it might be wiser for Andrew to attend £200-a-term Heatherdown in Ascot, near to Windsor Castle and highly recommended by a new member of the royal circle, Angus Ogilvy, now married to Princess Alexandra.

It was a regular sort of schooling. Maths with geometry and algebra, english, scripture and so on, with plenty of games in the thirty acres of grounds. Happily for the young tough, the school started its own scout pack and he learnt about knots, how to differentiate between a granny-knot and a reef-knot, how to cook such delights as 'twist' – a peculiar Scout recipe of flour, water and a touch of salt wrapped around a stripped piece of wood and cooked over an open fire lit with the regulation maximum of two matches. He enjoyed those days in the open air far more than he did his time in the classroom.

In the holidays, whenever possible, he ragged with Charles and Edward. The eleven years difference with Charles seemed unimportant, and little Edward, four years younger, could always be pushed around and made to run errands – it is hardly surprising that Andrew grew up to be such a beefy chap. He did a certain amount of horse-riding, and his sister Anne was keen to improve him. But just as she was the one to encourage him, she was also the cause of him abandoning it. He certainly was not the first younger brother to be temporarily discouraged in his horsemanship by a bossy elder sister.

It was Prince Philip, under the guidance of Lord Mountbatten, who initiated the move for Prince Charles to go to his old school, Gordonstoun, founded by the German Kurt Hahn to educate 'the whole man', near Elgin in Morayshire, Scotland. It was considered by many a bit *too* forward-looking to send the heir to the throne to a school open to all – or at least to those who could afford the fees – and particularly a school with such a hearty reputation, and the Queen Mother made no secret of her opposition. It wasn't the idea she was against, but the school. If she had fully realised the extent of the spartan regime she would have been even more opposed, for, as it turned out, Charles was an intelligent and sensitive boy and he had little taste for the tough life, for being ducked fully clothed in a cold bath or for any of the other schoolboy rituals.

There was a move in the family to send Andrew to Eton, the *alma mater* of Prince Richard of Gloucester, Prince Michael of Kent, and Princess Margaret's husband, the Earl of Snowdon. However, Charles having broken the mould, and Anne having gone, at her own suggestion, to Benenden, and Prince Edward having just joined his brother at Heatherdown, Philip felt that Andrew, who was not the brightest of scholars, would probably do well at

Gordonstoun. And, unlike his elder brother, Andrew did indeed enjoy his schooldays. Security was less strict than it had been for Charles, the life was easier and it was quite a different world from the Gordonstoun of the old days. As headmaster John Kempe says: 'We even had central heating and the swimming pool was heated to 75 degrees.'

The major change – and it was a big change – was that some of the 390 pupils paying £1,050 a term were girls, following the trend in many traditional boys' public schools. The previous year Gordonstoun had taken their first thirty boarding girls into the sixth form and another thirty were joining the third form at the same time as Prince Andrew. One of the most extraordinary things about that form was that one of the twenty in Prince Andrew's class, Sarah Alexander, had, the previous term, shared a form and a dormitory with Sarah Ferguson at Hurst Lodge.

Sarah Alexander was brought up in Kingston, Jamaica, where her father is an entrepreneur and real-estate dealer, and she explains: 'I'd been sent to England to be educated at Hurst Lodge – I had the strongest Jamaican patois accent when I arrived – and I was in Peach dormitory with Fergie. She was lovely and such great fun and I loved my time at Hurst Lodge, particularly all the dancing, and I made so many friends.

'Then, after two years, I heard that my cousin Deborah de Lisser, to whom I was very close, was coming to school in Britain and going to Gordonstoun. I said that I had to be with Deborah and I would run away if I couldn't be. So my father sent me to Gordonstoun in the middle of the year, in the same year as Andrew. I still kept up with my friends at Hurst Lodge and I used to get letters from Fergie when I must have been right next to Andrew.'

At Gordonstoun there was none of the standing on ceremony that Andrew was used to. The masters called him Andrew and he called them Sir. But no one could claim that he was just another schoolboy. His detective, who slept in the San – the Sanitorium block – was always on duty (the first one was replaced by the much-trusted Geoffrey Padgham after reports of gunfire in the school grounds, drinking, and the matter of the young biology mistress), and when he got an exeat to attend his sister's wedding at Westminster Abbey he was flown south from RAF Lossiemouth, which adjoins the school, in an Andover of the Queen's Flight. The school had a cross-section of people who could afford the fees and there were others who made fast getaways: it wasn't unusual at the school's only half-term, in the winter term, to see a number of helicopters land on the school lawn to whisk children, such as shipping millionaire's son Philip Niarchos and American Red Jones, off to London, New York or wherever, for the weekend.

Even at that age, according to a fellow schoolboy: 'He certainly let everyone know who he was and had a pretty high opinion of himself. He got away with a lot of little things that the rest of us wouldn't have, such as handing work in late.' These were the early signs of what a later commentator would call 'an unmannerly pleasure in his princely status'. Sometimes of course he used his princely status to good advantage and said what others have only thought, as when he commented in an audible whisper to the Queen Mother at a colour-trooping ceremony, when the Queen was asked for her permission to carry on: 'I do wish Mummy would say "no" sometimes.' And when, on another occasion at a Gordonstoun lecture on the future of Scotland under the Nationalists, unrecognised, he asked Scottish National Party MP Winifred Ewing what he should do if his mother owned a house in Scotland and a house in England. 'You'll just have to choose, lad. You'll just have to choose,' was her laconic answer. Gales of laughter greeted her innocent reply.

Another schoolfriend explains it: 'He was rather sad in some ways. He really didn't know whether he wanted to be a prince or one of the lads. The school was full of poor little rich kids and in some ways Andrew was typical of them. They'd make friends with one group for a term, two terms or a year, then they'd grow out of it and switch to another group. Nothing lasted very long.'

Andrew has always found it difficult to make real friends and to this day he has very few; the only ones he feels he can really trust are the hugely wealthy aristocratic relations that have been around the royal family since his childhood. But he did live a fairly typical life in Cumming House. He wore the grey long trousers, white shirt and blue pullover uniform and at weekends the needlecord trousers or the Gordonstoun kilt – Gordon's-town was founded by Robert Gordon, who allegedly sold his soul to the devil and, incidentally, had his own green-and-blue tartan which the school has adopted. Andrew would usually wear the kilt – 'There's nothing worn under it,' he once told a girlfriend, 'it's all in good working order.' On one of his parents' visits, a friend recalls how, unnoticed, he observed Andrew, wearing the kilt, and Philip walking together, hands clasped behind their backs, by the Services Centre assembly building where Andrew was about to appear on stage in a small role in the farce, *Simple Spymen*: 'They weren't saying anything, but they looked so alike it was amazing. And Andrew looked so proud of his father – and his father looked so proud of him.'

Although not as keen on acting as Charles, Andrew was still an enthusiast and also played Lucifer in an experimental outdoors production of Marlowe's *Doctor Faustus* on South Lawn, with a loud pre-recorded soundtrack that included music from David Bowie, Fleetwood Mac and Led Zeppelin. There were smoke machines, helium balloons and all manner of special effects for the three nights of the play's run and the actors wore grotesque, home-made masks of papier-mâché, chicken-wire and wood. As Keene Alexander, who played Gluttony, recalls: 'Andrew had a strong, dominating voice that made him ideal for this. We recorded all the voices on reel-to-reel tape beforehand and mimed. It was an amazing production, and very good.' Andrew joked about taking the story seriously, and putting on dark glasses, he would say: 'I'm invisible now,' before going off with his detectives.

If Andrew did exhibit signs of snobbishness – once

assistant headmaster David Byatt was asking a class what they planned to do when they left school and Andrew said, 'It's all right for me. I've got a job to go to already' (for which he got a hard time and a lot of teasing from his classmates) – he also joined enthusiastically in the school activities. For instance, at the age of fourteen he was one of fifteen Gordonstoun boys who went on a three-week exchange school trip to the Jesuit Caousou College in Toulouse where he stayed with a French doctor and his wife in the residential suburb of Balma. He told his hosts that his father was a gentleman farmer, his mother didn't work and that his name was Andrew Edwards, from his first and last Christian names. But a contemporary on the trip says: 'With his face, the detective and all the fuss, he didn't fool anyone for a second, but they all politely went along with him.' In London he said that his one ambition was to go to the cinema. The first few schoolfriends he asked to go with him turned him down, as they felt they would be embarrassed by the attention he would cause. It was some time before he did find a willing cinema-going friend to accompany him and explain the mysteries of queues, ticket offices, intermissions, popcorn, a feature film and those dire travel documentaries which the royal family escape.

Life was pretty innocent and Andrew already had, mainly from the guidance of his father, a highly developed sense of duty. He was aware that his position was different from the other pupils and apart from ragging about in form, he really did behave quite well.

All illicit activities, such as there were at Gordonstoun, took place in the woods around the school – Chapel Woods, Eve Woods, Plantation Woods, KG Fields, Airfield Woods (just by RAF Lossiemouth). But although Andrew did go with his pals on smoking expeditions – two cigarettes a week was considered really heavy smoking – he didn't actually smoke himself. The dangers if he was found out were too grave, expulsion was quite common for the mildest offences, and he had discovered at Buckingham Palace that he didn't like the taste of cigarettes (Princess

Margaret is the only smoker in the royal family) and he
didn't much like the taste or effects of alcohol. Most of all,
he didn't feel he had to join in to be cool.

There is one incident that may explain why, as he had
enjoyed Heatherdown, he also enjoyed Gordonstoun. Just
as he didn't smoke or drink, so, unlike most of his contemporaries, he didn't swear. One friend says that he can only
remember Andrew swearing once, when a girl asked him
what Buckingham Palace was really like. Andrew pursed
his lips. 'It's like a fucking prison,' he said.

While many in the school – except for the helicopter
crowd – had a long way to travel on exeats, Andrew had
Balmoral nearby. He once made plans to take about ten of
his pals to Balmoral for a brief break, but as he said, 'I'll
have to ask Mummy if it's all right.' Mummy said it wasn't
and that he was welcome to bring a couple of friends home,
but not a whole crowd. If Mummy had realised the teasing
the poor boy would have because of her decision, she
might, possibly, have changed her mind.

There is no doubt that the thing Andrew most enjoyed at
Gordonstoun were the girls. The homosexuality unsurprisingly found at the all-male schools of Charles's time had
disappeared, and Andrew was tall, good-looking ('My
brother's the one with the Robert Redford looks,' as
Charles once said with a touch of envy) and very attractive.
With an awful inevitability it did not take long for Andrew
to be nicknamed Randy Andy, in the way that all Whites
are Chalky and, for that matter, all Fergusons are Fergie.
Randy Andy was, like all the boys, inordinately interested
in girls although the randiness was more in thought than
deed.

Just as the healthy young teenage boys at Gordonstoun
were girl mad, so the healthy young teenage girls, in their
ultra-short regulation grey skirts, were boy-mad – a much
more satisfactory arrangement when the numbers eventually became more equal. But while Andrew could have
had the pick of the bunch, his tastes were a surprise to his
friends. One says: 'He never used to go for the prettiest

girls – and there were some stunners there who were keen on him. Instead he seemed to go for bigger, plainer girls.'

In fact Andrew's first girlfriend, Jenny Wooten, was in the sixth form. After that was Cally, Caroline Oldershaw, in his own form, then Kirstie Richmond, a very sweet girl but hardly rated by her peers as a great beauty. The 'romances' with girls were intense but innocent, mainly a lot of note-sending, hand-holding, meaningful looks and long kisses – going any further was for the more adventurous sixth-formers only.

In the classroom Andrew did not seem to be trying very hard and his main pleasure came from art, where the master Jim Wardell became one of his few confidants. Andrew, who has some talent as a draughtsman, felt genuinely encouraged and to this day spends his free moments painting – just as his father does.

When the O-level results were posted there was a mysterious thick black line through his results, although his classmates deduced by careful examination of the paper that he had in fact achieved just one pass. His father was not best pleased, and a stern lecture was delivered that made it quite clear that Andrew's Duty now was to pull up his socks, and pretty rapidly, too.

Someone in Andrew's position at Gordonstoun would normally go into Form 5T – T for Transition, where they could retake their O-levels before going into the sixth form. This would have been a major embarrassment, and an ingenious way out was found. Andrew would have some intensive private tuition from Christopher Trevor-Roberts, who had previously coached Charles, and he could further follow in the steps of Charles and spend a year somewhere in the Commonwealth.

Charles had gone to Timbertop, part of Geelong Grammar School in the foothills of the Great Dividing Range, about a hundred miles from Melbourne, in Australia, so, as a similar exercise and 'to broaden his experience', it was decided to pack Andrew off to Canada. Flying out first-class under the pseudonym A. Cambridge, in January 1977 he started a two-term stint at Ontario's Lakefield College in Peterborough, between Montreal and Toronto.

Some Canadians were surprised at the choice, as both Upper Canada College in the centre of Toronto or Trinity School College (TSC) in Port Hope, in the Kawartha Lake District about seventy miles from Toronto, could have laid claim to the prince. Ridley and Appleby are favoured by the rich, but Lakefield is known as a discreet establishment and, like Gordonstoun, it is a member of the Round Square Conference group of schools which propagate Kurt Hahn's principles of educating 'the whole man' and Andrew's visit was to be part of the exchange scheme operated by the sixteen schools in the group.

Andrew had been to Canada once before when he accompanied his parents and his younger brother Edward to the 1976 Montreal Olympic Games to cheer on Princess Anne as a member of the British Equestrian Team. And his father had visited Lakefield to present some awards there eight years earlier. Not everyone was pleased to see the prince, inevitably. The folk around Lakefield, more concerned with genuinely local issues – for instance, the local council had just passed an anti-noise ordinance which, according to some, would place a ban on birds disturbing people with their early-morning singing – were warm in their welcome, but the *Toronto Sun* suggested that it was patronising to the country for the royal family to send their son out to the colonies. It was to Andrew's credit that he acquitted himself well there, although Terry Guest, headmaster of the £3,055-a-year school, reckoned that it was a bit different from Gordonstoun, despite the similar uniform of blue trousers, white shirt and a V-neck pullover. 'The first practice for field games,' he says, 'usually consists of clearing up the snow.'

One of Guest's concerns was protocol, and he says: 'Our main worry was what the hell we were going to call him. So we had a staff meeting and came up with a scheme. The boys would call him Andrew, the staff would address him as Prince Andrew, the governors would call him Sir, and the chairman of the governors alone would give him Your Royal Highness.'

He shared a room with Dominic Grant, who had already shared with him on an exchange visit to Gordonstoun, and joined in enthusiastically, from ice-hockey (in which he had wisely also had some private tuition in London, and was adjudged 'quite vicious, which is what you need for the game'), to kayaking (it's mighty cold when you fall in) to playing the role of the sexagenarian Mr Brownlow in Lionel Bart's musical *Oliver* – although he did draw the line at singing. 'I'm really no good,' he said.

He toured the Rocky Mountains and went on a 300-mile canoe trip in the North-West Territories – sharing a canoe with headmaster Guest, 38, and they only failed to negotiate one lot of rapids, called Bloody Falls. 'We did get wet,' says Guest. 'Bloody wet,' was Andrew's recollection back in Britain. It was cold and tough, although according to the locals, the bear and wolves in the area would run far faster from you than you could from them, and the only real danger is from the huge black flies which, despite protective equipment, managed a large number of royal bites. Andrew left behind an imaginative view of Gordonstoun to give to Peter Dance, the sixteen-year-old Lakefield pupil who was to be the next to visit Gordonstoun: 'The beds are as hard as iron. It's straw mattresses and bread and water. It's just like prison. It may be colder in Canada but the beds are more comfortable.'

There were girls a-plenty in Canada and the only real problem Andrew faced was coping with jealous schoolfriends as the Canadians forgot any republicanism in their efforts to meet him. His favourite, frequent weekend companion and teenage sweetheart, was his schoolmate Sandi Jones, the pretty, blonde, pony-tailed daughter of retired Colonel Campbell Jones of Kingston, Ontario, who had been his host the previous year for the Olympics. When he returned to London with a party of friends, he took Julia Guinness to Annabel's in Berkeley Square, and had to wear a waiter's necktie as he didn't have one of his own.

Annabel's is not the most fun place for a seventeen-year-old girl, but it seemed frightfully grown-up to Andrew.

Relieved to be back at Gordonstoun, he shone in sport, captaining the Cricket XI (on a good day he's a useful batsman) and the Rugby XV, and performing creditably in swimming races. He was head of Cumming House as Colour Bearer (prefect) Leader of the sixty-one pupils in his house, but he never reached the heights of his brother and father and made Guardian – head boy. He was no brain-box but he did, according to the Palace, manage to get 6 O-levels (they didn't point out that this was 'eventually'), and 3 A-levels, albeit with straight Es – in english, economics and history, sitting the first two under a pseudonym and history under his own name.

Inviting schoolfriends home takes on a whole new dimension if they are girls and Andrew tried to make use of all his opportunities. Seventeen-year-old Kirstie Richmond, daughter of a widowed nurse, had spent the weekend at Sandringham and a night at Buckingham Palace. There were other Gordonstoun girls whom Andrew took around: in his last year there was Nassau-based architect's daughter Clio Nathaniels and, according to his contemporaries, another major fancy was American Sue Barnard.

He had got a taste for being airborne when he was in the Air Training Corps at Gordonstoun, and actually thought of joining the Royal Air Force, doing a parachute course at RAF Hulvington in April 1978. By December, however, he had decided to combine his love of flying with his father's service and took aptitude tests at the RAF Officers and Air Crew Selection Centre at Biggin Hill as a preliminary stage to applying to join the Navy in a twelve-year short-service Fleet Air Arm commission.

4

Green Blancmange and Nice People

It was as a toddler that Sarah Ferguson started her education in Mrs Laytham's kindergarten in Englefield Green 'for the children of the gentry' – that included children of the Lascelles family (Earl Harewood), the Haigs and of the Duke of Marlborough's sister, Lady Rosemary Muir – with the eventual plan that she would join her sister at Hurst Lodge School, in Charters Road, Sunningdale, near Ascot, conveniently near her home.

From the age of three Fergie was on a horse. Her mother was very keen and an excellent horsewoman, and right from the start Sarah was a good rider. 'Over the years,' says Major Ferguson, 'she rode at pony clubs, gymkhanas, junior trials and events – all that stuff. There was no great success but she was always there or thereabouts.' What he later remembered most about her riding was her courage. 'She was very brave. She used to go absolutely straight and take crashing falls and would sit on the ground beating the ground in frustration. Because she knew perfectly well that it was her fault she'd fallen off, not the horse's.'

The little girl with her bright curly hair and outbursts of angry frustration was given the nickname Ginger Bush by her father – over the years abbreviated to GB. In later years it could be misconstrued in the way that many childhood names are, and Ferguson, who had got used to it, never told other people of either the initials or the meaning.

At home to look after the two girls, in her striped cotton pinafore uniform, there was the young Finnish nanny Ritva – now Mrs Ritva Risu with two children of her own. While

Jane's hair was an auburny mouse, Sarah was always a carrot-top and Nanny Riva used to call her 'My little red hair'. Both girls were well-behaved and Nanny Ritva remembers that they never gave her any trouble: 'Sarah especially was as quiet as a mouse. Once her head hit the pillow she fell asleep.'

The two girls were very different. Nanny Ritva says: 'Jane was the more ladylike while I felt Sarah was more the tomboy. She had that personality and character about her. She was just so full of energy and had a great sense of humour. Yet Jane and Sarah always got on well together. They quarrelled sometimes over toys and Sarah would cry – but usually she got her own way.' Like all tomboys, Sarah's greatest joy was getting grubby.

It was Nanny Ritva who would take the two little girls to see their father play polo at Windsor and it was there that she – and Sarah – would meet the Queen and other members of the royal family. But even she admits that the first meeting of Andrew and Fergie is lost in the mists of time. She thinks that they must have behaved like all toddlers on first meeting: inquisitive, pushy, shy. Nanny also looked after the girls when their parents went off on holiday, sometimes mixed with business trips to France and America.

When, in 1967, Ronald Ferguson decided to move from Lowood House, leave the army and take over Dummer Down Farm in Hampshire after his father's death, Jane was coming up for ten and Sarah, now also at Hurst Lodge school, was seven. Reluctantly young Sarah and Jane said goodbye to their schoolfriends, although no one knew that it was not to be a permanent parting.

Outside Basingstoke stands the magnificent Daneshill House where Miss June Vallance ran her school for girls. The school took both boarders and day girls. Jane and Sarah were entered as weekly boarders. 'It was a wonderful school,' says Sarah's contemporary, Charlotte Blacker. 'There were only about sixty girls there – about twelve in each of the six forms.'

It was at Daneshill that Fergie first became widely known as Fergie. But she was not the first Fergie, as her sister Jane explains. 'I was originally called Fergie,' says Jane. 'But then later it somehow got so that a few girls still called me Fergie, while others called me Jane – I didn't have any other nicknames. Sarah got stuck with Fergie and everyone called her Fergie.'

The school holidays were packed with activities. Plenty of riding, swimming, and Fergie was an enthusiastic tennis player. In the winter the family would go off skiing to Courchevel, Méribel, Chamonix or Arosa. 'Her skiing is just like her riding,' says her father, 'she goes straight – bang – and always has done, not particularly elegant but dead straight. Jane, on the other hand, was much slower and more elegant. Jane was always tall and thin, Sarah is quite a different shape – be careful with that or else she'll kill me. Jane on a horse was the same, such elegance, but about a hundred yards behind Sarah. Sarah's a sporting girl and a tough girl.'

Unhappily for the contented Daneshill pupils, Miss Vallance's brother, who had an interest in the school, decided to sell the house. It was an unhappy day, and as the school was to move to a smaller site at Dogmersfield in Hampshire there was no alternative but to close the senior school – so the boarders suddenly had to make other arrangements. While this was a traumatic time for everyone, it was especially so for the Ferguson girls as it happened when their lives seemed to be collapsing owing to the chain of events set in motion by that fateful Greek island holiday.

When their mother announced that she was leaving Dummer Down House 'for a little while', the news came as a blow not only to Jane and Fergie but to their friends as well, for Susie Ferguson was a tremendously popular and glamorous figure among the horse-mad young Daneshill girls, to whom she used to give riding lessons at the weekends. So if there was shame for Sarah and Jane, it was different from what one might expect. The initial devastation was that their mother would no longer be organising weekend riding events. Another schoolfriend says: 'We really didn't know what was happening, or understand it. We were all horse crazy and what upset us was that we didn't go riding with Susan any more.'

Both girls, always a shade in awe of their energetic parents, became withdrawn and noticeably insecure. A schoolfriend reports: 'It was terribly sad. Fergie was very, very unhappy and unsure of herself. To have become like she is now is quite amazing, and I never would have guessed she would become so sparky. But I suppose Jane eventually got over it by getting married so young and moving away and Fergie got out of it by being so outgoing.'

The schooling problem was eventually resolved. While the other Daneshill girls scattered to the four corners, it was decided that the Ferguson girls would return as weekly boarders to Hurst Lodge.

Hurst Lodge had no great claims to academic brilliance – dancing was more its preferred pastime – but it was a cheerful and friendly place of about a hundred pupils, half day-girls and half weekly boarders, run by Miss Doris Stainer, younger sister of the film actor Leslie Howard, whom Ferguson had met when he had acted as military adviser to the film *Charge of the Light Brigade*. Miss Stainer was a Queen Mother-like figure who rather floated through the school, taking particular interest in the ballet.

So it was not surprising that the arts were so emphasised and that a number of actors sent their children to Miss Stainer's care, although there are few outstanding names from those times.

The feeling of the school is probably best summed up by Robert Morley, whose daughter Annabel was a popular pupil. It was the prize-giving ceremony of her last term and Morley, having presented the prizes (there were none for Annabel) and encouraged the parents to donate money for the planned swimming pool, said: 'When Annabel came here at the age of ten she was untidy, happy-go-lucky, disorganised and awkward. After five years of Hurst Lodge I'm delighted to say that she's untidy, happy-go-lucky, disorganised and awkward. Mercifully, Hurst Lodge hasn't changed her at all, for which I will always be grateful.'

Robert Morley's wife Joan says: 'That sums up Hurst Lodge exactly. It was a very happy school and Robert was very keen to find schools for the children that wouldn't change them. The extraordinary thing is that now Annabel is by far the most organised of our three children. Annabel discovered the way that she was remembered was by an art teacher who said to some of the girls: "If Annabel Morley can get O-level Art, then so can you."' Robert Morley adds: 'I was very pleased with the school.'

Among Fergie's contemporaries were Aimi McDonald's daughter Lisa Mulidore, Peter Finch's daughter Samantha Finch, Ted Rogers's daughters Fenella Rodgers (he dropped the 'd' for his stage name) and her younger sister Dena, bookmaker William Hill's daughter Miranda Baker, circus man Billy Smart's daughters Davida and Gabriella Smart and Fergie's special friend Florence Belmondo, daughter of Jean-Paul Belmondo.

The school building itself is unimpressive, a suburban between-the-wars house that has been endlessly added to with half-timbered and low red-brick studio extensions, with a mish-mash of four wooden shed classrooms outside. There are two tennis courts, the swimming pool (Morley's pleas were successful), the 'long room' with television for viewing at weekends and *Top of the Pops* on Thursdays. It's right next door to Sunninghill prep school but there is little contact between the two. There were occasional forays to the nearby Eton or Wellington, and once a year there was a performance of Handel's *Messiah* with Wellington College and some other local schools at Bracknell Sports Centre.

A few girls left Hurst Lodge with O-levels, and those with ambitions to go on to take A-levels would move elsewhere, as there was then no sixth form. Certainly there was no pressure exerted by the staff to push the girls along. They didn't play any of the hearty games, like lacrosse, normally associated with a girls' school, although Fergie was a great netball player (netball was played on the tennis courts in winter) and in time captained her house team – she was in de Valois, named after Doris Stainer's friend Dame Ninette; the other house was Howard. There were 'extras', like music lessons, ballet and drama, but Fergie didn't do any of those.

A contemporary, who was one of six in Peach dormitory – they were all named after colours – with Fergie, recalls those early days: 'My main memories of Hurst Lodge are the horrible grey uniform, grey pleated skirts from Peter Jones, grey pullovers, white socks, flat shoes and grey surroundings. That and macaroni cheese and fluorescent green blancmange, although it was sometimes pink. We all ate in the large dining-room and lots of the girls had cousins or brothers at Eton up the road. There was a tennis court, but very little sport, just lots of ballet, which I adored.

'At night in the dormitory there were pillow fights and we used to get quite hysterical about the silliest things. We talked about boys, and becoming an actress and things like that. There was only a hint of taking work seriously. It was a pretty ugly, uninteresting school dumped down in the middle of Sunningdale. Guffaws and Hoorays, that's it for me – but despite all that it turned out some very nice people and certainly Fergie was one of the best of the bunch.' In fact as long as a grey skirt was worn, there was total freedom (within reason) in other items of dress. No jewellery was allowed, except a cross or earrings for girls who had pierced ears.

Among the boys that Fergie talked about, naturally enough, were Prince Charles and Prince Andrew. Prince Andrew in particular was a source of great speculation and excitement, especially when Fergie was fourteen and her dormitory and classfriend Sarah Alexander announced that she would be going to Gordonstoun. The very thought of all those boys was sufficiently exciting, but the presence of Andrew made it doubly so and during Sarah's last term she got her friends to autograph an exercise book. There, alongside Florence Belmondo's 'Good Luck With The Boys!!', in flourishing misspelt schoolgirl script is written:

'Good Scotish luck!! Mind Prince Andrew lots of love
Sarah Fergie (FERGUSON) XXXX XXXX XXXX
XXX'.

When she was very young Fergie had been terribly
self-conscious of her freckles and her fair complexion,
going from the faded patterned-carpet look in winter to the
veritable explosion of freckles in the summer months.
However much people reassured her, young Fergie was
convinced that this was some great punishment from
above. She would even pray by her bed at night that the
freckles would go away.

For a young girl growing up, the problems of being a
redhead were tremendous. She couldn't go out in the sun
too much in case her fair skin burnt. Her red hair tended to
be coarse and unmanageable – full-bodied and strong
would be the polite way of describing it – going wavy and
frizzy when it was damp. And it was even worse when,
along with the other girls, she once had to wash her hair in
vinegar and water, following an outbreak of head lice at the
school.

As far as Fergie could see, the only benefit was that the
fairness of skin did cause the mistresses to be concerned
about her health and there were, it must be admitted,
occasions when she used this to good effect. But as one
friend reports, Fergie had one great advantage over most of
the other girls: she had a perfect, and spot-free complexion. The friend says: 'Most of us spent our time discussing
the merits of Estée Lauder skin cleanser but Fergie never
needed it.'

Fergie was a tomboyish figure throughout her schooldays, very slim and athletic. She was mad keen on horses
and would sit glued to the television during the *Horse of the
Year Show*. And when she was home at weekends she
would go for long country walks. 'We always seemed to
walk about eighteen miles or so,' says one weekend guest of
the Fergusons, 'but looking back I'm sure it wasn't quite
that bad. But I do remember in the winter Fergie opening
all the windows at about 7 a.m.'

'She loved midnight feasts in the dorm,' classmate Sarah Clapham recalls. 'One night we moved all the beds out into the assembly hall.' They were silly pranks, but as Sarah says: 'If we were up to something Fergie was usually behind it.' Fenella Rodgers, now Heron, a day girl who became joint head girl with Fergie says: 'We always had a laugh when Fergie was around. When I saw her poking fun at Prince Andrew on TV the other night I knew she hadn't changed.' And another girl says: 'If there was a cream-bun fight, Fergie would be leading it and she was terrific at making apple-pie beds. I remember once she filled a sugar bowl with salt and fell about laughing at the faces of the girls as they tasted it.'

Fergie was tremendously enthusiastic about everything and was hugely popular, especially among the younger girls – the ages ranged from four to sixteen – and was a frequent subject of innocent 'pashes'. As Lisa Mulidore says: 'Everyone looked up to Fergie, she was a great source of strength and fun. She was a great head girl for we all liked her.'

The dormitory conversations were naïve and innocent, as one of the girls says: 'ninety-nine per cent of the talk was about boys, and one per cent was about food.' What did they discuss about boys? 'It was all pure fantasy – we talked about boys we had seen in the holidays. Boys we had seen in films or magazines. We were terribly innocent. Fergie had seen *Tom Sawyer* in Leicester Square and had a crush on Johnnie Whitaker, who was in it and had red hair like her. We all called her Fergie – I only ever called her Sarah if I was really mad at her.'

Fergie had some difficult times, such as when her mother called at the school before leaving for Argentina. Fergie knew she wouldn't see her for six months, but hiding her real thoughts, she put on a brave face and stoically said goodbye. Her friends, knowing what was happening, were concerned and sorry for her, yet Fergie came back chattering animatedly about some school gossip as though nothing untoward had occurred. And yet, her life was falling apart.

She adores her father, but now, at such an important time for her, her mother had walked out and was going to the other side of the world. The only consolation and strength that she and Jane had was in each other.

Fergie threw herself with even more gusto into the life of the school: she became captain of netball and no one was surprised that when she reached Form 5A she was made a prefect. This entitled her to move to Little Hurst, the small wooden annexe to the main school overlooking the swimming pool, where the prefects lived and had a more comfortable life, with a small kitchen for making tea, coffee or toast, and a sitting-room with a television set. There she had a room with just two others – at first she shared with Florence Belmondo and Elizabeth Nightingirl, also from broken homes.

Fergie took her duties as a prefect and, later, as head girl (jointly with day girl Fenella Rodgers) seriously, and to this day one girl, who admits that she was a handful, recalls how, at the age of nine, she was expelled after she was seen walking out of the school grounds without permission. 'Fergie saw me and reported me,' she says. 'Although I suppose that incident might just have been thought of as the last straw, I was a bit wild, but it was for that that I was thrown out.' Yet her dormitory mates say they were, by their own accounts, one of the worst batches of prefects ever and Fergie was always larking about.

Liz Nightingirl recalls: 'There were awful dances "against" a local school – with us it was either Wellington, Radley or somewhere. I remember one Saturday we went to a dance at Bearwood College which was a bit like a cattle market, but we giggled our way through the evening. We were taken by coach and for most of the evening were left alone with the boys. The masters and mistresses were very brave to leave us as we were only let loose like this about once a year. The whole thing was rather embarrassing, though there was no alcohol so it was terribly innocent.' For a long time that night, no one asked anyone to dance. But if Fergie was a wallflower, so were all the other girls.

As a prefect Fergie had another task: every year at Halloween it was traditional for the prefects to set up a kind of pedestrian ghost train for the younger girls to walk through in the dark, while Fergie and the other prefects threw water at them, made scary noises and did their best to scare the poor girls witless. 'I'm sure that it was dreadful for the girls with a nervous disposition,' one of the perpetrators reports. 'But afterwards we had a buffet supper and party at which everyone had to entertain, while the prefects disguised themselves and for the best entertainment awarded a prize of a half-eaten bar of chocolate.'

The conversations in the prefects' dormitories were hardly more mature than in junior dormitories; they were about television programmes, films, marriage and how many children they would have – lots, preferably by a handsome, rich, prince.

Weekly boarders, who relied on the day girls for a constant supply of goodies, had to stay behind at weekends a couple of times a term to help with monitoring meals, shopping expeditions to Sunningdale (one sweetshop and a supermarket) and going to church on Sundays. Sometimes there were grander outings, like going to London to see *The Taming of the Shrew* (the set play for O-level English) at the Shaw Theatre in Bloomsbury, with Nicky Henson as Petruchio and Susan Hampshire, Henson's lover at the time, as Kate. Henson made a major impact on the girls, and as one of them reports: 'I have a note in my diary which says "Fergie and I have fallen in love with Nicky Henson."'

In her last terms at Hurst Lodge, while her sister Jane was having her big romance and getting engaged, Fergie moped to one friend about herself. 'I don't think I'll ever get married,' she said. 'I can't imagine anyone wanting me.' She didn't like her hair, she didn't like her face, and she thought her hips and bottom were far too big. There is a more positive view from former headmistress Mrs Celia Merrick, who recalls: 'From a very small girl Sarah always had charm, humour and a sense of fun. She had a very sunny disposition and a lovely smile. She was enormously cheerful, bubbly and fun-loving. She was not a superficial girl. But she also had a stubborn streak. I should think she will suit the young prince very well – she is a strong enough character to keep him in order.'

There was an annual midnight swim for the prefects in their last term. Fertile imaginations have suggested that the midnight swim must have been skinny dipping in the altogether. Not so. 'You must remember how innocent we all were,' one of the swimmers says. 'We wore things like T-shirts and jeans and bath hats. It was just a bit of silliness. We would have been expelled without a doubt if we swam naked. Sure, we talked about it, but we didn't actually do anything about it.'

The end of that summer term was particularly special, for it was the culmination of events for Jane Ferguson which had started some years before. At the age of eighteen, she was getting married to Alex Makim, the young Australian who had become a permanent fixture at Dummer Down by now. Alex Makim's cousin Belinda Coy had first come to help Susie look after the horses. Then Makim's sister Sally had appeared to look up her cousin and been invited to stay. Then Alex, a tall, tanned, 25-year-old, had arrived: he came to see his sister and he wanted to learn how to play polo. The fact that his potential polo instructor had a pretty, long-haired daughter just about to turn sixteen had quite an effect on Alex and his enthusiasm for polo. He was an enormous help and emotional support to Jane at the time of her parents' break-up. His breezy optimism was just what she needed to help her through, and it came as no surprise when Alex asked Major Ferguson if he could marry his daughter.

The Makims are a comfortably-off farming family and Ferguson was happy to give his blessing, although he did caution Jane about marrying at too young an age – Jane needed no reminding that her mother had been eighteen when she married her father. Jane took a secretarial course in London and then a cookery course while living at the First Street house with the housekeeper, but the house, originally kept on for the benefit of the girls, did not have happy memories and the final straw came when it was the victim of an IRA bomb. It was the time when the Price sisters were in Holloway Prison and a female prison officer was living in the house exactly opposite the Fergusons'. 'Thank God that Jane and the housekeeper, who had been watching television downstairs, had gone to bed,' says Major Ferguson. 'The thing had been left on the doorstep and the blast had gone downwards and completely wrecked the room where they had been sitting.' It wasn't long afterwards that the house in First Street was sold.

Jane completed her courses but had no desire to settle into London life – she wanted only to make a home with Alex, and on 20 July 1976, in the little village church of Dummer, just one month before Jane's eighteenth birthday and at the end of Fergie's last term, they married. Fergie, carrying a basket of flowers, was a bridesmaid. A reception for four hundred was held in a marquee on the lawns of Dummer Down House, before Jane and Alex headed off for their honeymoon and a new life in Australia.

Fergie felt more alone now than she had ever felt in her life. For not only was her mother living most of the year thousands of miles away, but now her sister, her closest friend and strength, had also left. As ever, she put on a brave face to the world. Still only sixteen, she had to try and piece together some life for herself. She had no notion of what would happen next. There were no big career-girl ambitions, just a desire for a happy life with no particular thought as to how that would come about. In the meantime, her only plan was to meet lots of people, make lots of friends and see the world.

5

Officer and Gentleman

At the age of nineteen Andrew followed in the footsteps of his elder brother, father, grandfather and great-grandfather when he went to the Britannia Naval College, Dartmouth, as a midshipman to begin his career in the Navy. He had had a taste of royal duty the year before when he had toured Africa with his parents, but now was the time to plan for his future and the Navy seemed to offer everything he wanted, from responsibility to a sense of purpose and free time enough for him to have some fun.

Andrew did have an advantage over his contemporaries as far as girls were concerned. He was good-looking, fit, amusing enough, enthusiastic, wealthy and a prince. On the other hand, this could sometimes work against him. Normally physical attraction comes first, other things come later. But with Andrew the fact that he was a prince could easily swamp the situation.

An occasional early date of the prince recalls: 'Just imagine the situation. Here was a healthy young man on a date with a girl. The first thing to remember is that there is a detective-in-waiting, if only outside the door. Do you kiss on the first date? And if you do, is it because you find him attractive or will he think that you're a gold-digger?'

'Andrew was very sweet, but he was terribly awkward and unsure of himself with girls. You can't blame him, can you? On the one hand he's got so much, but on the other hand that all gets in the way . . . We were never more than just friends – I really don't know what would have happened if he hadn't been a prince, but he is and you can't ignore that.'

While his early girlfriends had not been the prettiest of his contemporaries, when Andrew left school he more often found himself with glamorous girls who were prepared to make the first move. They, too, may have been shy but were armed with the professional veneer that is the stock-in-trade of actresses, models and royalty. And he quickly found that he was not averse to their attentions.

He met the perky and ambitious eighteen-year-old Miss UK, Carolyn Seaward, in 1979 when he was training in the West Country – her gentle accent gives away her Devon origins. She didn't know whether she was ambitious enough to catch a prince, but she certainly decided to investigate a bit further. One night they returned to Buckingham Palace after a night out and Andrew suggested they went up on to the roof. Now what is an eighteen-year-old girl to think of an invitation like that? Carolyn really didn't know, but she was aware of what that could mean in the West Country. So, in her long and clinging evening dress, out she went.

Andrew led the way up a metal fire-escape ladder. 'We always used to come here when we were children,' he said. Then they were on the flat roof and there was a skylight through which they peered: down below was part of the servants' quarters and the couple could see dressing-gowned figures preparing themselves for bed. When Andrew had done this as a youngster the servants had sometimes been well aware of the little eyes prying down, but this time Carolyn and Andrew looked down on the scene quite undetected. It took some time before their relationship went further.

Then there was the rangy, 5′ 10″ model girl, Gemma Curry, whom Andrew met when her RAF wing commander father tutored him on a North of England flying course in the summer of 1980. She accompanied him to Princess Margaret's fiftieth birthday party at the Ritz that autumn, provoking Carolyn Seaward, at home in Devon, to joke bravely: 'I'll kill him when I see him.' Through Gemma he met her 5' 7" cousin Kim Deas, whom he also dated. Then there was Carolyn Biddle, from a wealthy American family, whose sixteen-year-old sister was a friend of Viscount Linley.

It was theatrical impressario Michael White who introduced Koo Stark to Prince Andrew. White is a slow-talking but quick-thinking producer responsible for West End shows such as *Oh! Calcutta!, The Rocky Horror Show* and, in more recent times, the successful Comic Strip films for Channel 4, with a wide circle of glamorous and interesting acquaintances. His parties at either his South Kensington home or at 13 Duke Street, St James's, where he had offices with an apartment upstairs, were always an eclectic mix of showbusiness folk and horse-racing personalities, the type of arty and moneyed company that Andrew enjoys.

Koo, born Kathleen Dee-Anne and at first called Kitty Koo, is the daughter of American film producer Wilbur Stark and his TV actress wife, Kathi Norris. Her father, Wilbur Stark, whose film-making involvements have included *Cat People* and *The Thing*, has long worked on the fringe of big-time showbusiness and Koo came to school in England at the age of fourteen with the grand plan that she would return to America when she was eighteen after attending a Swiss finishing school. That was not to be.

Koo was seventeen when her father left London to return to the States, leaving the family to fend for themselves, and leaving Koo to offer to settle at £5.00 a month a judgement against him for non-payment of a £100.00 bill for removal of her wisdom teeth by Harley Street dentist Maurice Bliss. Koo did indeed mean to fulfil her pledge, although to this day she has not done so, and on her own two feet, took a starring role in the Earl of Pembroke's – he works in the film business as Henry Herbert – mild sexploitation movie, *Emily*, a kind of Emmanuelle look-alike, eventually going on to play small roles in *The Rocky Horror Show Movie*, when she met White, and *Star Wars*. She also made a low budget movie called *Cruel Passion*, very loosely based on the writings of the Marquis de Sade, in which she played a nun who undresses, spends a night in bed with another nun and finally gets eaten by wild dogs.

At the age of 20 she met Robert Winsor, then 36, a wealthy and star-struck manufacturer of advertising display items, and lived with him, on and off, for four-and-a-half years. Winsor was a lavish host with an opulent house called Highcroft in Totteridge, North London, set in four acres inhabited by flamingoes, penguins and other rare birds; inside could be found showbusiness types such as Bob Monkhouse and Des O'Connor.

He had been married twice previously. Firstly to model Tina Tutin for one year and then to former Miss Australia-turned-model and *Golden Shot* TV hostess Valli Kemp for eighteen months. Koo moved in, and seemed fairly settled, although they broke up briefly when Koo had an affair with Christina Onassis's ex-husband, banking heir Alexander Andreadis, then thirty-three, on holidays in Greece and St Moritz.

Despite Winsor's track record, Koo wanted 'the security of marriage' but the evening before the planned wedding at Barnet Register Office on 10 March 1981, Koo chickened out, announcing that she had to fly to New York urgently to visit a sick relative. When the dust had settled, Winsor was philosophical, reckoning that he might have had a narrow escape himself. His previous argument was that there had been no need to wed as he would always look after Koo if they should split up: he kept his promise and gave her £12,500 towards a flat and a £4,000 Mini GT.

Koo turned to her friends for reassurance and comfort, two of them being her model girlfriend Bea Nash, who offered her sanctuary, and who was the 'close friend' invariably referred to by the press. The other was *Rocky Horror* film producer Michael White. It was at a small party of White's that Andrew first set eyes on Koo. And straight-away he was smitten. She has a kittenish face and an air about her of needing protection – one of the features that led to her making some seventy-six TV commercials – which Andrew was keen to offer.

Koo preferred staying in at Buckingham Palace to going out on the town and it was not long before Andrew realised that he had found his first true love. It wasn't the puppy love, the hand-holding and groping romances of his early days but a real, physical, no-holds-barred love. In Koo he found a girl who liked him and wanted a physical relationship. Of course she was experienced, and knew how to please a man – there are few who can resist silk or satin underwear and silk stockings – but she was also caring, patient, understanding and thoughtful.

Andrew was literally bowled over. He could not believe his luck. For the first time a girl did not stop to consider his position but just treated him like a man. She has never spoken of their love or of their lovemaking and it is only through a later brief dalliance that the Koo-taught secret of counting aloud to give added stamina came to be revealed.

Amazingly they managed, by dint of using White's flat as a rendezvous and by taking elaborate precautions which only added to the excitement and illicit nature of the romance, to keep the affair out of the limelight until February 1982. For in Koo, Andrew had found somebody who was bright, ingenious and aware that if the romance came out the whole thing might be blown. And happily for him she did, and still does, genuinely care for him. The person in danger of giving it all away was Andrew himself, who wanted to share his new-found happiness, pleasure and maturity with the world. When it did surface, to the salivating delight of Fleet Street's prurient editors, Winsor offered a word of caution: 'Koo is a beautiful girl and very sexy. But she is also tenacious, jealous and as hard as nails. At twenty-two he is still an inexperienced lad and compared with me at his age he has led a very sheltered life.'

Andrew produced her for inspection by his family and the family seemed to like her. She went up to stay at Balmoral and behaved impeccably. Prince Philip approved of this poppet of Andrew's and rather wished he were a young man again himself. The Queen too seemed to like Koo – her liveliness, her brightness and her demure prettiness. But no one in the family thought that the affair would last long. The general feeling was that it was good for Andrew to get it out of his system.

Andrew certainly didn't spend all his time playing around and, just as he was taking his first really passionate affair seriously, so he was genuinely serious about the real responsibilities of his naval career. He'd been twenty-one when he had qualified for his wings as a helicopter pilot and had joined 820 Naval Air Squadron flying Sea Kings on the aircraft carrier HMS *Invincible*, starting to serve 'frontline' in October 1981. As he says himself: 'How soon it was that the designation Frontline became all too true and real!' For in April 1982 he found himself sailing south for the Falkland Islands.

6

War and Peace

The arrival of Argentinian scrap-metal dealers to dismantle a disused whaling station on the windswept Falkland Islands dependency of South Georgia in March 1982 provided just the excuse that the Argentine Government had been seeking to carry out their boast to the nation – the 'recovery' of the Islas Malvinas, as they still call that peat-bog-and-rock outpost of the Empire. On Friday 2 April, while Britain watched helplessly from 8,103 miles away, their troops entered Port Stanley.

There was no official declaration of war, but Great Britain inexorably found itself in deadly conflict with Argentina. The vast Task Force flotilla set sail, as the people of Britain held their breath and were convinced that diplomacy would solve the problem long before the fleet had made its long journey. In the air was that spirit of Jingoism – as the music-hall song had it: 'We don't want to fight but, by Jingo, if we do, we've got the ships, we've got the men, we've got the money too.'

As the inevitability of war, bloodshed and sacrifice loomed, there were many in Britain who felt a deep, sinking sickness: but none more so than Her Majesty the Queen. No one knew what would happen, but if the Task Force did reach the Falklands there was every chance that Prince Andrew, as the Prime Minister pointed out to her, would become a special target of the Argentinians.

The interview between Margaret Thatcher and the Queen was filled with tension. Two women, two mothers. But the Queen, the ultimate patriot, showed herself as strong as the Prime Minister. 'Prince Andrew is in the Navy and I am sure that he will fulfil whatever duties he is given,' was her message. There could be no suggestion that he was being treated differently to any other serving naval officer.

The Argentine nationals in this country shivered. They had no wish for the conflict. The whole operation seemed to be a morale-boosting exercise in their homeland to take people's minds away from Argentina's horrendous domestic problems. A piece of easy machismo, or so they thought. The Latin temperament is to brag more and do less: the English can be the other way round. There were plenty of reported speeches from the Opposition and elsewhere that suggested that the British would be a pushover.

Yet the lives of the cosmopolitan Argentinians, to whom the conflict appeared as an essentially local difficulty, were not particularly affected and Barrantes and Susie were able to live a quite calm existence on the estancia, looking after their horses and their land, worried mainly by the long-term effects of the conflict on the polo world, which was dominated by Argentinian players, horses and grooms.

In his forties, there would be no question of Barrantes, whose father was a retired army officer, being called up for army duty, yet he could already tell that this foolish and unnecessary conflict would change his life. Born an Argentinian, he could not completely forsake his country, however foolish its leaders might be. If only from a financial viewpoint the obvious future for Barrantes, who loved Britain dearly, was to find a new patron in the United States, and this he had done in Peter Brant.

When the 20,000-ton carrier HMS *Invincible* set sail with the Task Force on 5 April, most of the officers on board reckoned that they would soon be turning back for calmer waters: few believed that the Argentinians would not make a tactical withdrawal and some face-saving gesture.

But that was not to be.

There was much speculation in England that the Argentinians had marked out Andrew as a special target and that was why *Invincible* stayed some two hundred miles to the east of the Falklands, out of the way of immediate enemy action. That speculation was fuelled by the troops after they landed – to them, *Invincible* was an awfully long way from the sharp end of the war. This was nonsense. Andrew was not a priority target, but the two aircraft carriers were. The main priority of Task Force commander Admiral Sandy Woodward, stationed on HMS *Hermes*, was to ensure that the carriers were safe. They were desperately needed as the flying base and the loss of a carrier would have been a terrible blow for morale as well as for logistics. In fact, because of political decisions to run down the fleet, by previous Labour and present Conservative administrations, *Invincible* had already been sold for £175 million to Australia. The deal was hastily shelved, and indeed later rescinded.

Furthermore – and this was a major secret – for most of the campaign *Invincible* only had one propellor shaft operational; a gearbox failure had crippled the other. So the ship was not as manoeuvrable as it would be under normal circumstances, although Captain Black made light of the problem later: 'We did have a fault in our astern coupling, that is true, but that did not affect our forward speed and I did not intend to go into battle backwards.'

The reason that little was reported of Andrew in the war was quite simple and revealed one concession made because of him: while there were plenty of journalists on board *Hermes*, there were none on *Invincible*. Otherwise, under Captain Jeremy Black, a brilliant sailor, there were no concessions, except once. There was one particularly dangerous, almost suicidal, mission to cripple submarines on the Argentine coast. The Sea King would not have enough fuel to return to the ship, so the four-man crew would have to survive as best they could – they managed to ditch the machine and set fire to it on a beach in the officially neutral Chile, but were taken prisoner and spent the remainder of the war in custody. Because of the inevitability of capture, Andrew was not among those allowed to volunteer.

The general routine was dangerous enough and weather conditions were such that under normal circumstances the Sea Kings would not have been allowed up. And some of the casualties were caused by flying accidents alone. So it was a tough and difficult job he had. Around the Falklands, Andrew flew decoy missions, dropping metallic chaff from the helicopter to lure the Exocets away from the ships. He rescued the wounded from stricken ships, moved important supplies and acted as errand boy between ships and shore.

As the main Task Force correspondent puts it: 'He had a job to do and he did it. That's the best thing you can say about anyone out there. Hero is not a word I like anyway. Certainly there was no particular incident that happened that showed him to be particularly outstanding – but doing the job was quite outstanding enough.'

But of the 28,000 men who travelled 8,000 miles to war, 255 died and 777 were wounded – a casualty rate of 1 in 28, uncomfortably high odds by any standards.

For Andrew the worst part was when he was off-duty, in a deep sleep in his bunk, when there would be a sudden thump. He says: 'My cabin was directly below one of the helicopter landing spots. When I was tucked up in my bunk and the squadron was night-flying, every time one landed on the spot above my head there was an enormous bump as the wheels hit the deck.' He does admit that some landings were softer than others.

In the Falklands, like all the men, he wrote letters home. To his mother, to his father. To Charles. And also to the girls he knew. In the letters he could put down his thoughts. 'Of course I was frightened,' he recalls, 'if you're not frightened you make mistakes. When you lie down on the deck at that moment when there are missiles flying around, then at that precise moment you are on your own, and that's all there is.' But the greatest number of letters were to Koo, and there were plenty of letters back. He found the support of Koo surprisingly reassuring, he wrote. He had her photograph by his bunk. And in those long, lonely, dark nights and wild and windy days she was never far from his mind. He found that she came to mind at the most difficult times. But in true bachelor style, Koo was not the only one on his writing-list – he might, he thought, never be found out – and Carolyn Seaward was among the many old and new girlfriends who had letters from him. One officer reckoned that he must have had letters from every girl he'd ever met, and most of them got letters back from him.

Andrew spoke to his mother more than once. 'She was at home and she was surprised to hear from me,' he said, when, in time, an efficient communications system was set up. Priority of communication was sometimes wrong, however, as when HMS *Sheffield* was alleged to have been struck by an Exocet missile when the ship's defence systems were not operating properly because someone was communicating with London at the time.

Andrew is normally quiet about the real dangers and horrors that he faced in the Falklands, but just occasionally he has let slip the drift of his thinking there. Thousands of miles away from London and the courtiers, Andrew had decided in his own mind that he would marry Koo when he got back to England. It was a big game in the Mess among men and officers alike as to what they would do when they got back to Blighty. Most of them wanted to get back to the comforts of civilisation, and their loved ones. Those who wanted to break free from the restrictions they saw in their lives announced that they would definitely do so. Those with lovers and sweethearts said they would marry them, carry them off to some desert island and make love in the blessed and almost forgotten sunshine.

Andrew, as he always had done, was more inclined to keep his own counsel. But on more than one occasion he said: 'I don't know quite – I might even get married.' He never said to whom, but the broad grin that broke across his face when his fellow officers started to tease him and quiz him if he had anyone in mind made them all certain that he meant Koo. When he landed at Port Stanley he light-heartedly pronounced it 'quite a nice little town – the perfect place to spend my honeymoon'.

A considerable time was spent in the South Atlantic, in and around the islands, during and after the conflict. When the Argentinians surrendered in Port Stanley, there was a sense of loss and a desire to have some memory of those extraordinary times that made Andrew wish that he had a camera with him to catch the dejected soldiers, the mess, the grime, the chaos, the number of people milling around in different uniforms, most of them with guns.

On that blessed day – at 9 p.m. on the evening of 14 June – a huge sigh of relief went through the nation. All talk on *Invincible* was of when they would get home and what they would do there.

Andrew was to spend six months in all around the Falklands before he came back to England – he failed to get compassionate leave to attend the christening of his nephew Prince William, although he had cheered at news of his birth and there were drinks all round in the ward room. There might have seemed to be a down side to the celebration as Andrew was now pushed down to third in line to the throne, but he was delighted and said, 'Maybe now I'll be able to get some privacy.'

It was a right royal welcome when he did come back. Prince Philip in his full Admiral of the Fleet uniform sailed out in the Royal Barge with the Queen and Princess Anne to board *Invincible* at Spithead. When *Invincible* docked, Andrew, with one of the red roses handed to all the sailors between his teeth, strode down the gangplank and raised his hat in a cheer of joy and relief. 'It was an experience I wouldn't have missed for the world,' he said. How did he cope? 'A positive mental attitude. I told myself I was going to survive, I could say "by hell or high water", but I won't.'

There was an emotional reunion with Koo in London, when the couple could meet at Michael White's St James's flat, and his mother suggested that he brought Koo to Balmoral during his month's leave. They spent an idyllic time there, while he recounted to his parents every repeatable detail he could remember of his time at sea, told Koo all the unrepeatable incidents and took pleasure in the glorious countryside around the house. The Queen, in particular, was impressed by Koo – she was warm, bright and seemed to be obviously fond of Andrew as he was obviously fond of her.

All too soon it was time for him to join 702 Naval Air Squadron at Portland, Dorset, for six months piloting Lynx helicopters. He was promoted to lieutenant, appointed a personal aide-de-camp to the Queen, and having completed 600 flying hours he joined the 3,850-ton frigate HMS *Brazen* as their helicopter pilot – his helicopter was unsurprisingly named 'The Hussy', and when Selina Scott paid a visit to the ship Andrew, having so far failed to extract a phone number or a dinner date from her, did get her to autograph the nose of 'The Hussy' and add seven kisses, one for each member of the crew and an extra one for luck.

There followed a three-month tour of duty in the Falkland Islands, looking for Argentinian planes. There were no planes, just fishing ships and time to grow a naval beard. At the first opportunity after his return, he and Koo took off – flying economy-class (courtesy of the Queen) as Mr and Mrs Cambridge – an alias Charles had used, as had Andrew, when flying to Lakefield School – for the island of Mustique, where they would be joined by Koo's mother, Kathi Caruso, as she now was. Andrew fondly imagined that by having a chaperone no one would look askance at the holiday. Alas for him, that was not to be.

What should have been heaven turned into a nightmare. For a start, Andrew unwisely managed to travel on the same plane as some American reporters. Photographers and newsmen were crawling all over the place. The media chose to concentrate on Koo's brief appearances in softporn movies. In an extraordinary performance, the BBC TV *Nine O'Clock News* even concluded a bulletin with a filmclip of Koo naked. The camera panned down her body, and as it reached just below her waist the picture changed to the Welsh newsreader putting his biros into his jacket pocket and saying with a lascivious leer: 'That's all for now . . .'

In London the Palace were displeased. The Queen and Prince Philip were appalled by the coverage their son was receiving, and after a few fraught telephone calls Andrew decided there was no alternative but to abort the holiday. Dejected, he flew home alone – this time as Mr Newman. His younger brother Edward, who still does not fully understand the role of the media or the power of women, publicly hit out at the press: 'He came back from that holiday more drawn, more tired, than he did from three months at war. I think to treat someone who's just come back from serving his country like that is despicable.'

Despicable or not, the media attention had by now permanently sullied Andrew's relationship with Koo, making his grand passion seem to be something rather smutty. For all his time at the frontline Andrew, in the throes of his first great love, was still too emotionally immature to cope with that unpleasant reaction and it was becoming inevitable, although he would not admit it even to himself, that the affair must eventually end.

At the beginning of 1983, Andrew was again in the Caribbean, a blessed relief from the cold of the Falklands, to take part in naval and military exercises. He arrived in America on 18 February; just as Koo was due in the States 'to consider some film roles'.

'I flew over jungle, over Jamaica, the Bahamas and other beautiful parts of the world,' he recalls. 'In Belize I was partly responsible for flying a photographer around and once again I was made aware of a certain feeling of loss, because I did not have a camera myself.' Maybe it was as well that there weren't any cameras around as, during that time, he became entangled with an unfortunate and harmless, but embarrassing, incident with Vicki Hodge and a swimming party on a Barbados beach.

Vicki Hodge is one of the three daughters of Malta-based baronet Sir John Hodge, by his first marriage. Her elder sister Wendy is married to Lord Beaverbrook's polo-playing grandson Johnny Kidd and Vicki, always a lively girl, started a successful career as a model, after being a deb. In 1982 she was 35, divorced and had split from her former lover, East End actor John Bindon, recently acquitted on a murder charge. Vicki had stood by him during his traumatic period in custody, but the affair did not survive. The camera is not kind to models as they age and Vicki had little good work, so she decided to sell up and head for the Caribbean.

In Barbados she stayed with her sister's mother-in-law, Lord Beaverbrook's daughter Janet Kidd. The living is cheap, the sun shines and there is plenty of swimming. But her two problems were that she was impulsive and she had little money. The media has not treated her kindly: she's been painted as a bitch and a tart and, indeed, her list of claimed lovers reads like a *Who's Who* of showbusiness and includes Ringo Starr, Elliott Gould, Jaimie Niven, singer Gordon Waller, photographer David Bailey. In reality she is just a girl who wanted to have a good time. Those that know her believe there was nothing calculated in her seduction of Andrew.

In Barbados she and two English girls, 21-year-old Tracie Lamb from Haslemere and 26-year-old Lucy Wisdom from London, met Prince Andrew on shore and were invited to a cocktail party on board *Invincible*, which he had rejoined. Tracie was a bright and pretty girl and Andrew was not the only one to think it would be an excellent idea to meet up for a swimming party. After romping in the sea, with all of them tugging at each other's costumes, Andrew twice waved his maroon swimming trunks above his head, even, as he dived, exposing a patch of the royal bottom. Royal detective Steve Burgess, who thought a distant photographer was with a party of American tourists, said in circumspect defence: 'There is such a terrific underswell out there that it fills your trunks with sand and it's like having the Sahara Desert in your shorts.'

Tracie was the one who captured Andrew's attention, but later that day it was Vicki who managed to get him alone. And it was Vicki who teased him into making love under the palm trees.

Kissing and telling is never advisable; with the royal family it is instant death. So when Vicki told a reporter how she had been swimming with the prince, a phone call to Janet Kidd made it clear that the girls would not be welcome at any further naval events. Tracie was turned away when she arrived at the *Jolly Roger*, chartered by seventy officers for a farewell party for Captain Jeremy Black, now Admiral, and this time it was busty blonde hairdresser Jane Alleyne, 24, who ended up with Andrew in the Caribbean.

Vicki Hodge, who had been a useful newspaper informant in her modelling days, was approached by some Sunday newspapers for more details of the swimming party – even though at the time there was only the mildest hint that there was any story. *News of the World* editor at the time Derek Jameson decided it was of little interest and so the tale went to the *Sunday Mirror* for £40,000, which was to be split three ways between Vicki, Tracie and Lucy. The *Sunday Mirror* were amazed when they found what they had got, for Vicki is a straightforward girl and she told them the lot. They felt it wrong to print the full story and left out the details of Vicki's personal romp with the prince under the palms. It was some years later that Vicki, again short of money, resold the story to the *News of the World* – by then under a different editor – with more detail. For this she received £25,000.

The stories appearing in newspapers only made things more difficult and eventually it became impossible for Andrew to have more shore leave and to meet up with Koo on St Lucia.

Although Andrew has said that he didn't have a camera during this period, that wasn't quite true; he did have a small camera, but he started making inquiries in London about acquiring a more sophisticated system. Surprisingly he didn't consult his uncle, Lord Snowdon, but he took advice from friends and his inquiries brought him into contact with people involved in the photographic world. Eventually, in his search for a camera that would stand up to rough use and be capable of operating in both the poor and the very bright light he had found in the Navy, he decided to buy a steel-bodied Nikon FE2 from Wallace Heaton in Bond Street for £215, together with a Nikon 85mm lens for £295 and a 80–200mm Nikon F4 Zoom for £319.

Koo had become friendly with Norman Parkinson who had taken photographs of her for *Vogue* shortly after the Andrew/Koo romance became general knowledge. Now back from a session with him at his Tobago home, he suggested that she meet up with Gene Nocon, a 38-year-old Filipino-American who, with two partners, ran the Photographers' Workshop in the basement Studio D of the Floral Hall in Covent Garden. Nocon was educated as an engineer, had switched to printing eight years before and had gained an enviable reputation, working for Norman Parkinson, Faye Dunaway's photographer husband Terry O'Neill, Linda McCartney and others. He cares passionately about photography and knew that the public showed far more interest in average photographs taken by celebrities than in perfect photographs by professional lensmen.

At the time, Nocon was organising an exhibition of photographs of people who were themselves the subject of photographs, called 'Personal Points of View'. He'd already approached Zandra Rhodes, Griff Rhys Jones, Clare Park and, through Parkinson, Koo Stark. Andrew was well aware of the power that the Palace hierarchy held over him and everything he did and he explains his dilemma: 'Koo came to see me and suggested that I should take part as well. I replied that I was sure I wouldn't be allowed to.'

There then followed a strange game. Koo told Andrew that, without consulting him, she had gone to Nocon and asked if a friend of hers could take part. Andrew says that no names were mentioned and that Nocon was understandably doubtful about anonymous participants, yet agreed to see his work. But Nocon isn't stupid and it is only surprising

that Andrew swallowed the story. To Andrew's amazement and delight, no one at Buckingham Palace raised any
objection to his new interest and he busied himself in
sorting out material for the autumn show.

During the summer Andrew and Koo started to formu-
late a variety of plans. This, Andrew still believed, was real
love and it was difficult and frustrating for both of them to
have to hide their feelings. Their situation was not wrapped
in an historical context as the Duke of Windsor's had been.
Koo wanted to get married, but both realised the problems.
They did, however, hit on a solution of sorts. Koo would
find somewhere as a love nest for them and they should
continue as before, but with some public acknowledgement
of the relationship. That summer Andrew took many,
many photographs of Koo – from pin-ups, including the
tasteful nudes he could now develop and print himself in
the privacy of his darkroom, converted from a spare bath-
room near his room at Buckingham Palace, to formal
portraits.

But as the autumn progressed Andrew came to admit to
himself that he could never marry Koo. They still saw each
other as much as possible, wrote and spoke, but Andrew
had started the painful process of winding down the relationship. Koo still clung to the hope that something would
come of the romance, but she was intelligent enough to
acknowledge the warning signs and she was conspicuous by
her absence at the October opening of the 'Personal Points
of View' exhibition, where her pictures hung next to
Andrew's, as well as those taken by Nocon's six-year-old
daughter, Summer, London taxi-driver Malcolm Cleaves,
and eight-year-old Michael Legge. Andrew's pictures received rather reluctant praise from some and, as was only
to be expected, a deal of critical comment from others.

The romance between Andrew and Koo was at a low
ebb. There were an increasing number of lovers' tiffs.
The gunfire of the Falklands seemed a lifetime away
and Andrew was delighted when he was approached by
Ilford and asked if he would take photographs for their

1985 calendar – their story was that they were keen to use an amateur, particularly to feature black-and-white photography. Any expenses for models etc. would be met and an appropriate fee would be paid for his work. Prince Andrew naïvely leapt at the chance, and the company gained some excellent cheap publicity, and maybe even some exclusive photographs of royal homes or people.

There are certain things a prince can fix that might be difficult for lesser folk. For instance, Andrew dreamed up the idea of taking some shots of an office block, Griffin House in the Strand, empty and with its lights left on at night. There were various potential complications that were easily overridden. Firstly, the best vantage point was from the building across the road, the headquarters of Coutts, who just happen to be the Queen's bankers. Then permission was needed for models to pose – a girl under a bunch of mistletoe, for instance – in the empty building. Then a radio communications link from one building to the other was necessary for direction – that one is particularly easy if you have a couple of policemen with you. Finally, a quiet day was essential. Even though the quiet day they chose – Boxing Day, 1984 – must have been just about the most inconvenient possible for everyone involved, everyone co-operated to the full.

One incident in that episode appealed greatly to Andrew. When he was doing reconnaissance for the shot, he went to visit Coutts Bank. There was a group of four who were met by the managing director. They exchanged a few words of greeting before entering his office and turning out the lights to get a better view across the street. As Andrew regaled his friends: 'We got some very weird looks when we came out again.'

Ilford also got their exclusive royal picture: a magnificent fisheye view of the inside walls of Windsor Castle that was used on the calendar cover. (A fisheye lens has a tremendous width of vision: Andrew's cost £591.95.)

But the real bonus for Andrew was that he would need to

find some pretty girls to use in the photographs. It is always difficult for a prince to meet new girls, but here was the perfect opportunity. Andrew certainly made the best use of it.

The girl under the mistletoe was Kate Rabbett, 21, whom he had met at the Photographers' Gallery and had taken her phone number.

The girl in a shimmering black dress loaned by Zandra Rhodes was actress and dancer Finola Hughes, 22, who in 1984 became the first girl to visit Prince Andrew's new quarters in Buckingham Palace – the rooms previously used by Prince Charles.

Top model Clare Park, 27, whom he had met at the exhibition as a fellow photographer – she had taken some rather good nude figure studies, with no head visible, of herself, had advertised Oil of Ulay and Ryvita on TV advertisements and gazed through gauze for Andrew.

Clare, daughter of a retired British Airways Trident captain Keith Park, had gone from Guildford High School to become 'The Vogue Face of 1977'. She had given up dancing when she had hurt her back and, like Gemma Curry, was on the books of an agency called Models One. For a while over the winter of 1984 Clare visited the prince at Buckingham Palace in his second-floor rooms overlooking Birdcage Walk, St James's Park, the bedroom dominated by a large four-poster. Flowers from Andrew arrived at Clare's Hampstead home, and she dined at the Palace, but while she was happy with that arrangement Andrew liked to go out on the town. He is no great dancer, but was more than happy to end an evening out with a visit to Tramp discotheque in Jermyn Street. Clare was discreet and sweet but not what he was searching for at that time.

He was taking his work for Ilford with great seriousness, devoting all his shore leave to photographing, printing, and experimenting. There is often a relationship that develops between photographer and model and some even refer to the *droit de photographie* – the right of the photographer to sleep with the model, along the lines of the medieval *droit de seigneur*. So it was not surprising that when Andrew was seen in public with any of the girls he was photographing, they were immediately dubbed as Royal Popsies.

Kate Rabbett, who had posed under the mistletoe in Griffin House, was the 23-year-old daughter of gynaecologist Robert Rabett. Known to friends as Katie, or The Rabbit, she had lived with dancer Alan Curry for two-and-a-half years, and some discreet nude photographs of her did turn up and were published by the *News of the World*. That invariably puts the kibosh on royal girlfriends, but she did host a 24th birthday party for the prince at her Castlebar Road home in Ealing. Their relationship was unusual in that there was, at first, little in it. It was only after the media had named Katie as the new girl in his life that Andrew suggested that maybe they should do something about it. But it was never a relationship that would last and, in the background, Koo was still around.

During late 1983 and early 1984 Andrew and Koo met occasionally and spoke frequently, and Koo was still his closest confidante. In particular they discussed their latest photographic projects: the publishers Jonathan Cape had approached Laurie Lee to write the captions for a book of Koo's photographs, to be called *Stark Contrasts*; Hamish Hamilton wanted to publish Andrew's Ilford calendar pictures. But Koo was an increasingly sad figure. She hadn't been working much as an actress, as directors reckoned that her face was too recognisable and she was too well-known as an adjunct to Andrew to be taken seriously by audiences. She'd been offered tacky jobs, and bundles of money to 'tell all'. But that was not what she wanted. What she still sought was some security. Someone to love, someone to love her and a home of her own. She is something of a loner and can be intense about her feelings, and as the relationship cooled and she realised that it was coming to an end, her suffering was the greater.

There was the frequent pain of having to see Andrew's well-documented social life and she was at a particularly low ebb, filming for her book in the beginning of the summer, when she met Tim Jefferies. He was 21, the grandson of Green Shield Stamp founder Richard Tomkins, and he had inherited £500,000 on his birthday. He had a burning desire to be a racing driver and had already bought three Ferraris when he turned up to model for Koo at the Stock Exchange in May. Unsurprisingly he was quite taken by her, more surprisingly she went out with him. Within two months they were engaged, despite some objection from Tim's mother Hilary who said: 'I don't want him to marry her. Who wants such shop-soiled goods in the family?'

It can only be conjecture as to what Koo genuinely wanted when she told Andrew that she planned to marry. Whatever her feelings, within three months of meeting, Koo, 28, and Tim, just 22, were married by the Rev. Christopher Neil-Smith at St Saviour's, Hampstead, with just a handful of friends present. Tim wore a lounge suit, Koo looked stunning in a classically glamorous white suit. Neil-Smith, well known as an exorcist, had given Koo guidance and advice at several private sessions beforehand and it seemed as though she might at last have found some security. After a reception at the Savoy Hotel, they planned to make their home at a converted forge in Surrey.

Koo had trouble with her book. Her first publisher, Jonathan Cape, had rejected the project after Laurie Lee had turned down the commission to write the captions and Koo had not delivered any photographs of Andrew. She did eventually find a publisher and the book was published by Bantam Books a few weeks before Andrew's calendar was launched at the Photographers' Gallery – with a party attended by a number of Andrew's flames, including Carolyn Herbert, 22-year-old daughter of the Queen's racing manager Lord Porchester, Katie Rabett and Clare Park. Also present was Bea Nash – but not Koo Stark.

It was not long before Andrew had a hardback memento of his work; *Photographs*, published by Hamish Hamilton, which included the calendar shots and some other material he had taken and was launched with champagne at the ancient Stationers' Hall in the City of London. The photographs were interspersed with commentary by Andrew, re-written by literary agent Giles Gordon – who also handles the work of Prince Philip and Prince Charles – and then, re-re-written by Andrew. 'I want it in my own words,' he explained to the publishers.

By the end of November 1985, after just a year, Koo Stark's marriage was in trouble. Jefferies was young and too immature for Koo, who, although she had seen a chance of security with him, was eventually so exasperated that she moved out declaring that she needed some space and time to think. She went to see the Rev. Christopher Neil-Smith, who had performed the marriage ceremony, and he offered counselling and to carry out a full exorcism of the spirit of Andrew in Koo. She did not take up the offer. Instead she called Andrew.

Not surprisingly, those girls credited in the list of royal romances continued to flourish away from the limelight:

Carolyn Seaward was cast as a James Bond girl in the film *Octopussy*, spent a year with the Saudi Arabian Prince Sultan Al Saud, moved to a flat in Kensington and then back home to Devon. With judo expert Paul Redgrave she was credited as co-authoring the book *Self-defence for Women*. Then she went out with 27-year-old Swiss banker Laurent Mathysen-Gerste until, in mid-1985, he moved back to Switzerland.

Kim Deas, Gemma Curry's cousin, married adman Robert Barclay and remains a busy model.

Carolyn Herbert married Newmarket bloodstock, John Warren, and has settled down to raise a family.

Katie Rabett complained that her friendship with the prince made it difficult for her to get work as an actress, made a pop record that disappeared without trace, reverted to her proper name of Catherine Rabbett, dated *Coronation Street*'s Brian Tilsley (actor Chris Quinten) and surprised her friends by getting engaged and married to the extravagantly camp cabaret *artiste* Kit Hesketh-Harvey, 28, a former head chorister at Canterbury Cathedral.

Clare Park retired from modelling in 1985 and planned a new career as a photographer.

Vicki Hodge continued her simple life in Barbados, spending time deep-sea fishing for marlin.

Koo Stark's ex-lover Robert Winsor married and then split from black singer Grace Jones. He then sold Highcroft, complete with flamingos, storks, albino wallabies and penguins. Grace claimed that, among their other problems, was Koo's relationship with Winsor.

Koo moved to a Belgravia mews flat and, despite the comment on *Stark Contrasts* from the National Portrait Gallery that the best photographs in the book were the ones on the front and back covers, taken by Norman Parkinson and Terry O'Neill, she started work on a new book of photographs. She tried to revive her acting career. And occasionally she would speak to, and see, Andrew.

7

Getting A Job

When Susie Ferguson first went to Argentina she and
Hector Barrantes lived in Buenos Aires, before moving to
the little town of Trenque Lauquén, some 300 miles to the
south-west of the capital. To start with she found life rather
difficult in the Argentine. Although she was welcomed as
Hector's new wife, she knew no Spanish – the Argentinians
talk a particular version of Spanish, more a dialect – no one
except Hector spoke English, and he wouldn't translate for
her. 'For months,' she says, 'I was forced to sit and listen
instead of joining in conversations. Hector would not
translate for me because he knew I would have to learn the
language in order to enjoy Argentina.' She very soon learnt
to speak as rapidly as the natives.

In May 1975 they returned to England for the English
polo season and to see Sarah and Jane. Susie's relationship
with the girls had noticeably, if subtly, changed. They still
loved her, but they couldn't help but remember how she
had gone away before. It was almost as if, because she
hadn't been around to confide in or to row with, they were
now her friends rather than her daughters.

In England Ronald Ferguson had found solace in his
polo and his farming. He tried to make things easier for the
girls, but they remained introspective and withdrawn. It
was quite natural that Ferguson should want female company around the place, not only for his own comfort, but to
help care for Jane and Sarah. But rather than easing the
situation, his girlfriends only made it worse as the two
youngsters could not help but resent the intrusion of outsid-

ers into their world. If they didn't have a mother, they did at least want their father to themselves and now they didn't have him either. It was a sad situation as, in his rather awkward way, he was trying to do the best he could for them.

Ronald Ferguson's decision to look for another wife was an almost conscious one, as though it was his duty. As it transpired, he made a happy and fortunate choice in an atmosphere where love could quickly grow. As a single man he was in demand and his friends all tried to persuade him away from his life in the country. It was at a cocktail party in London that he met Susan Deptford, the 28-year-old blonde daughter of a prosperous Norfolk farmer, William Deptford, who had come to the party with her flatmate. Ferguson asked her out to dinner, but she declined as she was already committed to have dinner with her regular boyfriend. But Ferguson persisted and eventually she succumbed; 'it took a bit of time,' he says, wryly.

He and Sue Deptford got on well and she liked the countryside and eventually went to stay at Dummer Down House. Sue worked as a private cook for parties, christenings and dinners, and prepared lunches for the Bank of America in London. As soon as Jane and Sarah realised that this girlfriend was not going to be here today and gone tomorrow, they got on with her too. But the girls still looked for some means of escape from the unhappiness they had lived through. At eighteen, Jane would find security in her engagement to Alex Makim and marriage on the other side of the world; Fergie found her escape in the bubbling, extrovert character who would soon descend on London.

It took Ferguson some time to make up his mind that it was a good idea to remarry. By then it was almost a formality and Sarah and Jane reckoned they knew about the marriage quite a bit before their father proposed to Sue. It was in May, just as Susie and Hector returned, that he announced his intention of marrying again, but it was not until November, when the wedding at Dummer of Jane and Alex Makim was long past, that Ronald Ferguson married Susan Rosemary Deptford at Chelsea Register Office in the King's Road, London, with his mother and Susan's father acting as witnesses. She was 30 years old; he was 45.

Now that they were married Sue was keen to have a family of her own and she didn't have to wait long. At the Royal Hampshire County hospital in Winchester on 7 September 1977 Ferguson's first son, Andrew Frederick Victor John, was born. This was followed by the birth of Alice Victoria at the same hospital on Boxing Day, 26 December 1980.

When Fergie left school in 1976 she naturally gravitated towards London, to join the Sloane circuit – a peculiarly British phenomenon whereby expensively educated young girls come to town, attend a secretarial college or cookery school before taking a succession of usually short-lived jobs, working for publishers, public relations firms, or art auction houses, interspersed with skiing holidays, work as chalet girls or cooking directors' lunches. During that time they lead a frantically hectic social life of cocktail parties, dinners and occasional dances before finding and marrying a suitable mate in the same milieu. In fact, some of the jobs become quite responsible and it is a mistake to think that all the girls who follow this trail are not bright; but they very rarely start with the thought of making a career for themselves.

Fergie's father gave her a royal blue Volkswagen Golf car as she set off for London and in January 1977 Fergie started a £1,000, nine-month secretarial course at Queen's Secretarial College in Queensberry Place, South Kensington. There were many girls there from a similar background and Fergie made a particular friend in Charlotte Eden, daughter of Tory MP Sir John Eden, who remembers: 'We were joint bottom of the class. We were dunces at shorthand and typing. We used to sit at the back of the class and giggle, we just couldn't help ourselves. Fergie is very bright but she wasn't meant to be a secretary.'

Otherwise life was a great social round of parties, lunches, outings and weekends, with Fergie's enthusiasm for life exploding around town. She completed her course in December that year with final results of 90 words-per-minute shorthand and 39 words-per-minute typing. In the book-keeping exam she got 87 per cent. Her report described her as 'a bright bouncy redhead. She's a bit slap-dash, but has initiative and personality which she will use to her advantage when she gets older. Accepts responsibility happily.'

Having only a small allowance from her father and another small allowance from a trust set up by her grandfather, Fergie realised that she would have to get a job, but that need was temporarily postponed by a visit with her father to Jane and Alex at their 8,000-acre property, Wilga Warina, near North Star, on the New South Wales and Queensland border. In English terms 8,000 acres is a vast amount of land. In Australia it is not. The land is poor and some cattle stations reckon to have one animal to every two acres of land. Many of the larger cattle stations are owned by big conglomerates, large landowners in England or America, and are run by local managers, and life in the outback is hard for any farmer, no matter how well-off. There is irrigation, but little water. The rains come infrequently and often there is severe drought which stretches everyone to breaking point.

At the wooden house that is home, Jane had got things as well organised as possible. She and Alex had even managed to organise some polo, forming the North Star Polo Club at the tiny township (a shop, a petrol station and a pub) where they could play from May to September: Jane was the Secretary. Alex also played polo at Easter in Sydney, where his parents lived, although, as Jane says: 'We should plant our crops before May, if the rains do come, but we don't play any polo until we've got the crops in – that's the most important thing.' Wilga Warina has cattle, wheat and sheep – barley and early wheat, too. For Fergie it was lovely seeing Jane again, but there was nothing about the

Above left Sarah Ferguson learning to swim, taken from the Fergusons' family album (*Syndication International*)

Above right Prince Andrew, aged five, standing to attention (*Rex Features*)

Below Good Scotish luck!! Mind Prince Andrew. Lots of love Sarah Fergie (FERGUSON) – aged fourteen to a friend leaving Hurst Lodge to go to Gordonstoun, Prince Andrew's school (*Tim Satchell*)

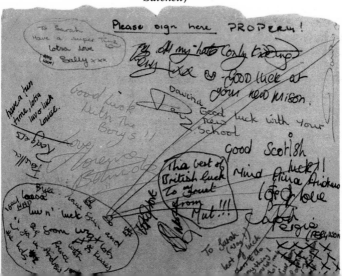

Above The sport she knows so well! A heavy rainstorm won't prevent Fergie from watching polo at Windsor in May, 1986 (*Rex Features*)

Below left Facing the cameras on the slopes at Klosters, Switzerland (*Camera Press*)

Below right At the Chelsea Flower Show on 19th May, 1986 (*Rex Features*)

Above left At a pro-celebrity shoot arranged by Jackie Stewart
near Chester, North Wales (*Alpha*)

Above right Returning to Portsmouth from the Falklands War
aboard HMS Invincible (*Alpha*)

Below Speaking to the crowds in Canada (*Tim Graham*)

Above   The kiss (*Camera Press*)

Below   The engagement ring: an oval ruby set with ten drop diamonds as a cluster ring in yellow and white gold (*Camera Press*)

The official engagement photograph: H.R.H. Prince Andrew and Miss Sarah Ferguson in the blue drawing room, Buckingham Palace (*Camera Press*)

Above   The bride and groom leave Westminster Abbey
(*Glenn Harvey, Camera Press*)

Below   The Duke of York kissing his bride on the balcony at
Buckingham Palace. The rest of the Royal Family from left: Mrs
Hector Barrantes, Prince Edward, the Queen Mother and the
Queen: *children from left:* Peter Phillips, Lady Rosanagh Innes-
Ker, Zara Phillips, Laura Fellowes, Prince William (*Martin
Cleaver, The Press Association*)

The Official Wedding Photograph: The Duke and Duchess of York at Buckingham Palace (*Albert Watson, Camera Press*)

Above Princess Diana and Fergie aboard HMS Brazen visiting Prince Andrew who had just returned from military exercise (*Alpha*)

Below Andrew and Charles: at the Guards' Polo Ground, Windsor Great Park (*Camera Press*)

lifestyle, except for Jane's contentment in marriage, that appealed to her.

Back in London, while her father became involved with his new marital life, Fergie threw herself into the social round.

Her very first job was a temporary one, working as an interviewer for Wendy Stewart-Robinson's Flatmates Unlimited, which she had started in 1971 and since built into a group of companies that included Babysitters Unlimited and London Domestics Ltd, based at 313 Old Brompton Road, South Kensington. One of the main helpers had become ill just at the time that Wendy was having her first baby. 'We were in a state,' she says, 'and we put out feelers for a person plus and via the bush telegraph we found some names and I interviewed a few and we chose Fergie – she was super and just right for the job.'

It was intended to be for just a few weeks but the job lasted around three months, then, through an introduction from her father, Fergie went to see Neil Durden-Smith, husband of TV commentator Judith Chalmers, at his public relations company Durden-Smith Communications in Basil Street, just off Sloane Street in Knightsbridge, made a good impression and was taken on. And it wasn't long before Fergie in her turn also introduced Charlotte Eden, who'd been doing a cookery course, to the fifteen-strong company.

Fergie started at £80 a week (it rose to £100) to work as a secretary on a group of accounts under Peter Cunard, an easy-going, smartly efficient executive, and she was made particularly responsible in her time for consumer accounts that included Ladbroke Hotels and the Seagrams drinks group with their G. H. Mumm champagne subsidiary. She arrived each day from her flat in York Mansions, Prince of Wales Drive, overlooking the south side of Battersea Park, where she had lived since leaving Queen's College, in her royal blue Volkswagen which she left on a parking meter – and which had to be fed every few hours. Some reports say she had a Mini, but her father says, 'I wouldn't give her a Mini. I don't think they're safe.'

Fergie was never short of admirers but her first regular boyfriend was Kim Smith-Bingham, a 6′ 3″, prematurely thinning Old Etonian who worked for a commodity broker in the City. Smith-Bingham is the son of racehorse owner Charles Smith-Bingham, a prep school friend of Ron Ferguson and the younger brother of Denis Smith-Bingham, the man who persuaded David Niven to go to Hollywood. Denis was a diplomat who had been a partner in David Niven's financially disastrous American Pony Express Racing Association (the plan was to use polo ponies out-of-season for racing) and, after writing to Niven about life in California, fixed him up to stay at the home of the young actress Loretta Young – the start of a famous career.

But Kim was not, by all accounts, blessed with the charm of Niven's circle. Two years older than Fergie, he had been considered somewhat arrogant at Eton, a mite loud, sporting a flashy blue blazer and a Panama hat, moving with a self-opined fast set and running up extravagantly large bills with Mrs Moulton at Tap (the Eton tuck shop – most bills were £15–£20 a term, Kim's were an almost legendary £60–£70). Nevertheless, he and Fergie became a regular twosome.

Most of Fergie's socialising was in the form of dinner parties and cocktail parties: some smart, some not so smart. She had gained some variation on her nickname in her new world of PR: there she was Fergie-poo and Fergs, but, as in her schooldays, she was never known as Sarah. As her boss Peter Cunard remembers: 'Sarah was a delight. She fixed up meetings – or rather, on occasions, forgot to fix meetings. She entertained clients, and was generally very good at her job. She was also always cheerful and happy. PR can be a job with plenty of ups and downs and there are plenty of young people around who can be moody – but never Fergie. She was always jolly. She was never bitchy, never involved in politics. If I, or anyone else in the office, felt a bit low, you could always go and have a word with her and you'd soon be cheered up. She was a joy to have around.

'She knew how to present herself and never wore anything that was remotely unsuitable. Like the other girls, she always wore a skirt, as we didn't believe in trousers for girls in the office.'

It was a small, friendly and cheerful office. After work, Fergie would go to Mossop's Wine Bar in Mossop Street for a drink with Charlotte Eden and other girls from the office, and to meet boyfriends. Or else they would go to the Carlton Tower Hotel Rib Room Bar for Happy Hour, when drinks were half-price and champagne was served in large mugs at £2 (the hotel is now called the Hyatt Carlton Tower and their Happy Hour is no more, alas). Her colleague Judy Regis remembers: 'Fergie always liked those gatherings. But she was incorrigible and couldn't stay still for long, she always seemed to be going to about five different drinks parties in an evening. She was always tremendous fun.'

She worked on several major projects, including a Young Chefs' promotion for Seagrams at the Dorchester Hotel. But if she presented herself as an assured and attractive young woman in her work there was one new problem in her life. With no netball, few games of tennis, fewer long walks and a sedentary life with occasional expense account meals she found she started to put on weight. So, if it wasn't a business lunch, it was invariably cottage cheese and cucumber, or, for a short time, the Grapefruit Diet, Scarsdale Diet or whatever the fashionable diet was at the time. Sometimes the girls in the office would go to the downstairs salad bar of Upstairs Downstairs, to the Basil Street Hotel's Parrot Club, a £10-a-year ladies' luncheon club convenient for shoppers and suchlike. In hot weather they would take sandwiches for an *al-fresco* lunch in Hyde Park and a spot of sunbathing, although Fergie would keep in the shade.

When clients were entertained in the office, Fergie was in her element and when, at Christmas-time, the staff – minus boyfriends and girlfriends – took over the Sale E Pepe restaurant in Pavilion Road, or a room at the Hyde Park Hotel, she was the life of the party. At the slightest excuse – birthdays, leaving parties – there would be champagne in Neil Durden-Smith's office. Durden-Smith says she was 'Marvellous. Great fun' and another colleague describes the office as 'the happiest place I have ever worked'. It wasn't the kind of office rife with petty jealousies, illicit affairs and rows – it wasn't big enough for a start and everyone was far too busy getting things done. 'I remember Fergs,' says one, 'as being like a particularly nice labrador around the office, very endearing. Very warm. Fairly naïve in a business sense, but always fun.'

The one drawback for Durden-Smith Communications was that Fergie spent an inordinate amount of time on the telephone, to her father, to her friends, and arranging her social life. But as long as she was efficient in her work there were not too many objections to that and Fergie was the kind of girl who had plenty of contacts around the place, so she did earn her wages.

A fair amount of telephone time was also taken up with Smith-Bingham, with arrangements, disagreements – and the problems and rows are still remembered. Her father in particular was not enthusiastic about the prospect of Smith-Bingham joining the family. Then something happened that would change the situation entirely, for Smith-Bingham found the pressures of handling large sums of clients' money uncomfortable and had decided to leave his City job and move to Verbier in Switzerland, where he became, in local parlance, a ski bum – that covers almost any excuse for doing as much skiing as possible; in fact, he was working for American Dale Anderson's smart skiwear company Ski Service, which allowed him time to indulge his passion for skiing. Fergie went out to Verbier to spend a month's holiday – the first of several – with him.

For Fergie, this was her first real adult relationship and she was determined to make the best of it. Verbier has some of the best skiing in Europe, with lifts going as high as 3,328 metres to the top of the Mont Fort glacier, and Fergie was an enthusiastic skiier and adored the après-ski life. 'She's very good,' says Smith-Bingham, 'black run standard. We had great fun.'

There were lots of Britons there – it sometimes seemed like an extension of Fulham with the invariably well-bred, hard-working and badly-paid chalet girls who cook, clean and look after the inmates of chalets for the pleasure of free skiing and the occasional on, or off, piste romance.

In the summer, out of season, Smith-Bingham would come back to England to spend time with his family and with Fergie. Otherwise, Fergie led an active social life in London, but was always totally committed to Smith-Bingham, even though her friends thought him a Hooray Henry type.

Sarah's relationship with Smith-Bingham lasted two years. Towards the end the romance cooled but they remained friends and in latter days she would cook supper for him, or they would go dutch at one of the sprouting South London restaurants. And he has maintained a gentlemanly aloofness since she has been in the public eye, although he does admit: 'We never talked about marriage. We were both too busy and too ambitious to think about settling down. Eventually I was in Verbier while Sarah was in London. We just drifted apart – it was a question of living different lifestyles. No one else was involved.'

'Neither of them was ready to settle down,' as one friend says. For her twenty-first, her father gave a cocktail party for a hundred and fifty friends in the Crystal Room at the Berkeley Hotel, with a dinner for thirty afterwards. Some of her friends had held grand dances, but Fergie didn't want that. 'Thank heavens,' her father said, with reference to the many thousands of pounds such an event would have cost. After the party, her father suggested that she might like to travel to South America to see her mother. Fergie leapt at the idea, and in the autumn of 1980 she left Durden-Smith Communications – more parties – and flew out to Buenos

Aires, before making the 300-mile journey out to Trenque Lauquén.

Susie and Hector had found an estancia of about 3,000 acres of rough, flat, and sometimes flooded farmland outside the town of Tres Lomas – Three Hills – in the province of Salequeló. There is a last twenty miles of rough track from the town to El Pucará, 'The Fortress', the Barrentes' simple, A-framed wooden house, with its incredibly basic facilities which eventually included a radio telephone that crackled and fizzed mightily but did establish a link with the outside world.

Fergie helped them move in, and Susie recalls that everyone fell in love with her. 'Naturally,' she says, proudly. Hector agrees. 'She has *chispa*,' he says, 'spark' in Spanish. She rose enthusiastically to the challenge of turning the basic dwelling area, not much bigger than a bungalow, into a home. As for the farm land, which was mostly boggy and in danger of flooding, Hector's first plan was to plant some 600 trees, and plough 100 acres to create a polo field, and exercise space for the ponies he would be breeding.

Susie, already universally known by the neighbours as 'La Inglesa', remembers the creation of her new home with affection. 'After Hector had finished clearing the land, he stood up on the tractor and pointed out to me where the trees would be and how it would look – and it does. You have to have a wonderful imagination to foresee that.

'We all worked together to create a home. It is one mile from the gate to the house and we planted the weeping willows, the spruce trees, and the cactus ourselves.'

Supplies have to be fetched by a bone-rattling twenty-mile drive to Tres Lomas and, until a year ago, this was also the nearest source of an international phone – and you can't make a collect call from Argentina, either.

Charlotte Eden, Cha as Fergie calls her, came out to join them for Christmas and recalls: 'It was a lovely Christmas, really quite traditional.'

The time in Argentina eventually came to an end and,

with a limited supply of cash that had to last a long time, the two girls headed north by bumpy bus up through Brazil to Mexico. Says Charlotte: 'It was pretty rough. We had a guidebook and used to find all the cheapie places to sleep. We had our bus and air tickets but by the time we got off the bus at Iguza Falls (on the borders of Argentina, Paraguay and Brazil) we'd run out of money. So we slept at the bus station on the benches. Slept isn't quite the right word. We were up most of the night.

'The next morning we were hungry but we knew what to do. In those places when you go into a bar they automatically put down a small plate of cheese. So trying to look as prosperous as possible we sauntered into a nearby hotel and asked for two glasses of water. They brought the water and put down the cheese. We scoffed the lot and ran.'

There were many nights when they couldn't change their clothes and the whole exercise was carried out on the tightest of budgets, as they travelled by Greyhound bus up the California coast to Los Angeles. They stayed with friends, and friends of friends, and finally made their way to the ski resort of Squaw Valley in the Lake Tahoe area where they skied for two months, earning extra money by doing odd jobs, looking after young children of other visitors, working as maids and even, quite illegally as neither of them had Green Cards, working in a bar.

Then they were off again by bus down to the South, crossing the southern states to Florida where they could meet up again with Susie and Hector at the Palm Beach Polo Club before heading up the East coast to New York and, in May, flying back to London.

Charlotte Eden, now Charlotte McGowan, remembers: 'They were marvellous, crazy times. We'll always think of them as tremendous fun – some of the happiest of our lives.'

Back in London Fergie had to find herself a job, to find somewhere to live and to catch up with her social life. The first major event she was due to attend, of course, was the wedding in July of Prince Charles and Lady Diana Spencer, to which she had been invited with her father.

She found the job and the home quickly. In the time-honoured tradition, through friends, she knew Carolyn Beckwith-Smith who had just bought a ground-floor flat in Lavender Gardens, just off Clapham Common in South London, and who was looking for a flatmate. Then both Fergie and Charlotte Eden found jobs as assistants-cum-secretaries working for art dealer William Drummond, a tall, fair-haired man of many years' experience in the watercolour field – and it was he who discovered a Constable oil painting that had been bought at Bonham's auction rooms and sold it to the Tate for £100,000. Charlotte was based in the Bury Street gallery while Fergie worked between there and the gallery that Drummond had at the time in Covent Garden. When he closed the Covent Garden gallery, because of the high rates, Fergie found another job working for the small independent video production company VIP, who were based at offices next to the Iranian Embassy in Kensington High Street and just opposite the Royal Garden Hotel.

In the middle of all this had come the invasion of the Falklands and war with Argentina. Sarah was among the many who watched with mounting horror. She knew countless people who would be caught up in the battle. There were Guards officers, naval officers like her friend Prince Andrew whom she felt she knew so well through her friendship with Charles and Diana and, worst of all, her mother and stepfather.

The polo world shivered, and at the outbreak of hostilities Ferguson was umpiring at the Palm Beach Polo and Country Club in Wellington, Florida. 'It was a difficult time, there were lots of Argentines playing there,' he says. Along with other sportsmen, from footballers onwards, the Argentine nationals had no choice but to keep their heads down, leave Britain and rethink their lives. Hector Barrantes headed back for his estancia and kept as low a profile as possible.

It was an agonising three months while rumours and Exocets flew around, far too near for comfort. But at last the battle was over. There were more political changes in Argentina and there was a tremendous sense of relief when Fergie finally talked, via a crackling phone line, to her mother.

Fergie was enjoying her work for VIP. There were many different projects, one of which was to make a half-hour video film called *The Wonder of Harrods* which was planned to be sold in store to foreign customers. Fergie negotiated a fee of £500 for Sheridan Morley to do the voice-over commentary, which they discussed over lunch at the Terrazza-Est restaurant in Chancery Lane, off Fleet Street. Morley says: 'She was terribly efficient; it was filmed at night when the store was empty – it looked quite magnificent and she was great fun to work with and I got paid straightaway.'

Unfortunately, Harrods, who had been dealing with a massive production by Thames Television at the time, were not particularly interested in the VIP film, cannot trace any details of it, and VIP went bust before any copies went on sale in the store.

Fergie used the time she now had to go skiing again and to look for something else. She saw Smith-Bingham although the relationship was by now platonic, and it was in Verbier that she met Paddy McNally. They had met briefly some six years before when Fergie was a rather awkward schoolgirl, but the new Fergie, bursting with vitality and fun, was quite a transformation.

McNally was a widower, 43 years old and with two young sons, Sean, then aged eleven, and Rollo, aged eight. Of medium height and not particularly good-looking, McNally is capable of being a man of great charm. His wife, 'Twist' (he claimed that the nickname for the former Anne Downing came from the fact that 'she's always getting her knickers in a twist'), had died of cancer in 1980, although she and McNally had already separated. Twist had met McNally when he was a reporter on *Autosport* magazine and their marriage had been made comfortable by her money – her father was racing-driver turned Monte-Carlo-based businessman, Ken Downing. Twist had continued to live at their Lausanne home and McNally often stayed in Chelsea at a small bachelor flat shared with racing driver John Watson. The Downings' attitude towards McNally has always been uncompromising: they have barely spoken since Twist's funeral, as they believe that McNally deserted her at the time when he was most needed, although he had been with her at the Capital Hotel in Knightsbridge when she was very ill and seeking treatment two years earlier.

There have been a number of misconceptions about McNally. He does not and did not manage Niki Lauda. He does not and did not work for McLaren International. However, he did work, until 1985, for the cigarette firm Philip Morris's Marlboro offshoot in their Lausanne-based sponsorship department, setting up deals, organising the drivers under contract – including Lauda. Before that he worked on *Autosport*, bought a share in Road and Race Services in Holborn (later in Fulham) which supplied serious driving equipment such as fire retardant suits, and raced his collection of classic Ferraris. He also raced saloon cars before joining the Philip Morris sponsorship department. His sons now go to Stonyhurst College, a Roman Catholic public school, and he divides his time between his Geneva apartment, his shared château in Verbier and the international motor-racing circuit.

Paddy McNally is a man with many contacts and friends throughout the world. His brother Peter is finance director of London Weekend Television. Paddy McNally is also a man with a roving eye. He had admired the big, bright and bubbly Fergie from a distance and decided that she would be his next conquest.

It was not long before Fergie became a regular fixture at the large chalet, Les Gais Lutins (the cheerful imps), he shares with property man David Elias in Verbier, a short drive up the hill from the town. The eight-bedroomed chalet is sometimes referred to as The Castle because of its

size and although McNally says: 'I have a strict house rule
that no one who has anything to do with drugs is allowed to
stay with me' some have even called the chalet Cocaine
Castle. Certainly there is an alleged occasion when Sarah
got quite angry after someone arrived bearing a frozen
chicken with some cocaine hidden inside it.

Parties at The Castle are famous and guest lists would
include many of the names that can be found in London
gossip columns: Jamie Blandford, the Duke of Marlborough's drug-troubled son the Marquess of Blandford,
entrepreneur John Bentley, his Daneshill-educated ex-
girlfriend Lulu Blacker, Nigel Pollitzer, manager of the
aristocratic pop group, The Business Connection, and the
group's lead singer Bunter Worcester, the Duke of
Beaufort's son the Marquis of Worcester, among many
others. Pollitzer, adopted son of the late George Pollitzer
of the industrial combine Beck & Pollitzer, is known as The
Rat or Ratty; McNally is known as Toad. Fergie coped with
all of them and made them at home. The chalet lent itself to
parties, with garages underneath, a large playroom and a
huge balconied room upstairs, with a fireplace and sitting
area at one end and large pine table in the dining area at the
other end, adjacent to a spacious kitchen.

After late nights, the guests would ski, lunch at the
upstairs south-facing balcony of the restaurant at Ruinet-
tes, or the more discreet Chez Dany further down the
mountain, meeting up with others in the evening at Hôtel
de Verbier, La Luge or the Mont Fort pub.

The nights would invariably end at McNally's regular
table at the Farm Club discotheque, run by Italian brothers
Giuseppe and Stefano in the basement of the Hôtel Rho-
dainia. The Farm Club is decked out rustically but, at 21
Swiss Francs (around £7, but you do get one free drink)
entry and 160 Swiss Francs (£50) for a bottle of whisky or
vodka (the preferred drinks), is not cheap. The discotheque is lively, but the floorshow among the customers is
often better. One habitué recalls recently seeing a waiter
calmly empty an ice-bucket over the head of one offending

customer – smuggling your own whisky in a hip-flask is considered a particularly heinous crime.

Fergie had met the former Formula Three racing-driver, Richard Burton, socially in London and in 1984, when he planned to set up a London office and was looking for someone to run it, her name was mentioned. Burton had managed racing-drivers Jackie Stewart and Joachim Rindt when he had retired from racing himself, and had then dabbled in property before setting up BCK Graphic Arts as a Swiss-based printing company and Richard Burton SA as a publishing concern. Fergie leapt at the chance and established herself in the tiny fourth-floor offices in St George Street, Mayfair, which had been ceded by Sotheby's – the building adjoins their offices – organising printing and publishing schedules. BCK does everything with particularly high quality – and high prices, publishing many catalogues for Sotheby's in New York and the Impressionist catalogues for Sotheby's in London, among others. The Tate Gallery, National Gallery and Christie's also use BCK. The relationship between the companies is close but Fergie actually works for Richard Burton SA, not BCK.

Fergie's job as *directrice* was as a London rep and sales girl whose job was to keep the existing clients happy and to get new ones. Being a one-woman office she also had to do the hoovering, typing, open the mail and make the coffee – that was when she didn't get a take-away cup from Queen's Café across the road. She had some indirect contact with her friends in the royal family when BCK became involved in publishing a catalogue of the Queen's collection of paintings at Windsor Castle. She was also in touch with people such as her old PR boss Peter Cunard, now working at Granard Communications under the umbrella of the Grandfield Rork Collins agency (since taken over by Saatchi & Saatchi). But as Cunard said: 'Fergs, old fruit, you're way too expensive for us.'

Fergie adored her new job and one of her first tasks, for which she was credited, was to liaise with everyone concerned with *The New Painting*: *Impressionism 1874 to 1886*.

This was a lavishly illustrated, 512-page colour production with a commentary by Charles Moffatt, Curator of European Art at the San Francisco Museum, which to date has sold 140,000 copies at between $20 and $60.

'We don't mind what hours she works, as long as she gets things done – which she does,' says BCK boss Burton, and Fergie, now well settled in the ground-floor flat at 40 Lavender Gardens, Clapham, loved the work, zipping around town in her new metallic blue BMW 316, a two-door model, registration number LVP 331X, which her father had bought from his stepfather, Sir Thomas Elmhirst.

Clapham, South London, is a pleasant, leafy area of Victorian suburban houses, often referred to as 'Cla'am' out of suppressed embarrassment or inverted snobbery by the smart youngsters who live there and who would far rather be living north of the Thames in Chelsea or even Fulham but who invariably can't afford to. From a minus point of view, it is a bit too close for comfort to Brixton, scene of the 1981 street riots, but it has reasonable shopping facilities (there is a Sainsbury's at Stockwell and another at Vauxhall Cross), there are plenty of local wine bars and restaurants which have opened up to cater for the new inhabitants, and access to the West End and Chelsea is good. As one neighbour says, with an air of disparagement: 'This place is just crawling with those Sloane Rangers now.'

Fergie heartily dislikes being described as a Sloane Ranger, that species first identified in *Harper's and Queen* magazine (the Sloane 'bible') by Peter York and Ann Barr, and protests that she isn't one. But she does show some of the classic signs, from her clothes, to her skiing, to living south of the River, to working in an art-related business in Mayfair and driving that ultimate Sloane and Yuppie – Young Upwardly-Mobile Person – car, the BMW. But is she a genuine Sloane Ranger?

Author Peter York is in no doubt: 'Yes, Fergie is a Sloane. She measures up to all the criteria of Sloanedom. There are of course different types of Sloane. The grand, the less grand, the aristocratically inclined or not, the exemplary Sloane, the upper-middle-class, the rich and the not rich.

'With Fergie you have the grandness through her family, and the relationship to Princess Alice, Duchess of Gloucester. You have the richness. Of course 800 acres of farmland in Hampshire is not seriously rich, but on the League Table of the Rich it definitely counts as rich. Not super-rich like the Spencers, but rich enough. It's certainly better than the Old Rectory with five acres.

'The next question with a Sloane is "Are they exotic or not? Are they stolid and solid? Do they have bolters in the family? Are they groovy? Have they been around in London?" Fergie certainly fits into the exotic. She may not look an obvious exotic, but her mother bolted with an Argentinian. She's been an international playperson, with McNally, and she's been mixed up with L'Équipe Anglais (the fast skiing crowd in Switzerland – not necessarily as fast, or as fun, as they would like others to believe).

'In fact she is really more typically Sloane than Diana. She is loud and jolly. She might push you in the ribs. She's really a pretty generic Sloane. I think she'll be a tremendous inspiration to all and a splendid role model Sloane.'

Meanwhile her father's polo-playing world had adapted itself to the Argentinian conflict. No longer did the Hired Assassins come to England and the supply of Argentinian ponies had dried up overnight. There were those – usually the less wealthy or the more careful, like Prince Charles – who bred and brought on their own horses. But there were others that started to arrive from Mexico, Brazil, America. And the players came too. From New Zealand and the countries of Central America. With them they brought the back-up supplies, the grooms and new enthusiasm. Some say that it has been the making of the polo world; one player reports: 'It really opened up the chances for the British. Before, you just couldn't compete with the Argies, but now it's possible for British grooms to get a job, for

British players to come to the top and for us to breed our own horses. In some ways it was a damn good thing.'

Fortunately for them, Hector Barrantes and the other Argentinian professionals did not suffer too much financially, as they could switch their playing to the profitable American circuit. Here polo is a game played for pleasure by the aristocracy and old money, aided by the professionals and with a smattering of new money; in America, where the prizes are high and the money is more plentiful, it is a game played for the prizes by the very wealthy aided by the professionals. So Barrantes started a new régime, whereby he would go to the States to play for the hugely wealthy Peter Brant for the months of January, February, March and June, July and August. Between times he would return to the estancia where he would look after the land, supervise the breeding of new polo pony stock and take a handful of young Americans as unpaid apprentices to learn how to care for horses and how to play the game.

Barrantes plays for the White Birch team with Brant, who created the huge Bato paper manufacturing company whose two paper mills supply newsprint around the world, including much used in the UK: last year White Birch won the World Cup at Palm Beach with Brant himself (handicap 5 goals) taking ('Quite undeserved,' he says) the Most Valuable Player Trophy. The two polo players met in England in 1979 when Brant played with the Vesteys' Stowell Park team and Brant persuaded Barrantes to play in America before the Falklands war. Afterwards it was natural that they should play together again (Barrantes plays off 7 goals in America and 6 in Argentina).

Brant says that reports of a vast salary paid to Barrantes are incorrect. 'He and Susie are dear friends,' he says. 'They come and stay as house guests at White Birch Farm, which is just next door to the Greenwich Polo Club, and I buy five or six horses a year from him, that's the extent of any financial arrangements between us.'

Major Ferguson decided that, until the Falklands conflict was officially at an end, it would be wisest not to accept any more invitations to umpire at the Palm Beach Club in case there was any suggestion of bias in an onfield dispute in which Argentinians were involved. In Britain the Guards Polo Club and others said they wouldn't let the Argentinians play here. The official reason given was that hostilities between the two countries had never formally ceased, but, as Ferguson confided to one friend, his own interest was more personal: 'I don't ever intend to let them come back. One of them ran off with my wife.'

In 1983 Paddy McNally left Philip Morris to set up his own business, specialising in circuit advertising. He knew enough about the cash involved on the international circuits to realise that, if he could do a deal with Bernard Ecclestone, boss of the racing controllers Formula One Constructors Association, he could have a flourishing business.

His relationship with Fergie flourished on the good days and floundered on the bad. The good news was that Fergie got on well with his sons, looked after them and acted as an efficient and always obliging châtelaine. The bad news was that while Fergie was looking for a long-term commitment and a serious relationship, McNally was not. And he had a habit, which annoyed others as much as it annoyed Fergie, of over-flirting with other girls, even when Fergie was around. Somehow, in the hope that things would improve, she tolerated McNally's roving eye, although others felt desperately sorry for her.

For, she said, the good times were very good and McNally could be generous. He called her Lollipop for she loved sucking things and as a present he gave her a gold chain which she could be seen wearing around her neck. On the chain hung two large gold letters: G–B, which McNally had chosen for her father's nickname. 'What does it stand for?' asked her friends. Fergie would giggle. 'Ginger Bush,' she replied.

Fergie's friends still came from all worlds, and among those she had become very close to in London were Vanessa and Dai Llewellyn, the latter at one time known as a playboy, considered NSIT – not safe in taxis – brother of Princess Margaret's friend, Roddy Llewellyn and son and heir of Olympic horse-riding gold medallist Sir Harry 'Foxhunter' Llewellyn. When their second daughter, Arabella Dominica, was christened at the Roman Catholic St James's Church in George Street – just next door to BCK's offices – Fergie was, for the first (and certainly not the last) time, made a godparent along with Countess Bismarck, Llewellyn's best man Michael Dupree and Princess Caroline of Monaco's husband, Philippe Junot. There was obvious glamour in that list, but Fergie was not there for her status: she was the 'respectable' choice, the totally reliable and nice one who would care for the child in any eventuality.

And that year had a very happy ending, for, her sister Jane and husband Alex arrived from Australia with their young son Seamus to spend his fourth birthday, on 17 December, and Christmas with the family, and, for Seamus to meet his grandfather and Aunt Sarah for the first time.

8

Best Friends

Under the vast dome of St Paul's Cathedral five years ago, on 29 July 1981, among the many well-wishers at the wedding of Prince Charles and Lady Diana Spencer were some close friends of the prince: his polo manager, Major Ronald Ferguson, his second wife Susan and his daughter Sarah. And it was that day that presaged the events that were to lead to another marriage. The marriage of Andrew and Fergie was to be the culmination of Major Ferguson's career and a triumph for Diana.

When Diana had changed from being invited to Balmoral as an adjunct to her sister Sarah Spencer, with whom Charles was having a passionate affair – in the early days of the Charles and Diana romance it was assumed by outsiders and insiders alike that the eighteen-year-old Diana was there as a friend for Prince Andrew – she was thrown into a new world and needed as many friends as she could get.

Apart from her flatmates Carolyn Pride, Virginia Pitman and Anne Bolton, and a few old schoolfriends, there were not many she could hope to call close friends among the new people she met with Charles. There were few she warmed to and few that immediately warmed to her – indeed, some were quite dismissive as they had different plans for Charles. But one of those in Charles's circle to whom she did warm was Sarah Ferguson. Diana was just starting the remoulding process: out must go the rather timorous Lady Diana Spencer and in must come the Princess of Wales, a future Queen for the King of England – an awesome role indeed. And in her new life one of the greatest and strongest friends she made was Fergie.

There were a number of reasons for this. As the Princess of Wales, Diana had to draw the core of her new friendships from among Prince Charles's circle. She might, in time, be encouraged to make her own friends outside this circle, but that would not be for a while.

Major Ferguson was already close to the prince and a trusted adjunct to the court so it made sense that the Ferguson family would be around and equal sense that their daughter Sarah, unmarried and, like Diana, not totally enthusiastic about the playing of polo, should become her frequent companion on the polo field.

Although Fergie is almost two years older than Diana, they got on famously from the start. At a vulnerable age both had been left by their mothers, who had gone to live far away. Fergie is unpretentious and enthusiastic and has a natural gift for making people feel relaxed. So close did they become that Fergie was the only non-family member invited to the small, private birthday lunch at Buckingham Palace for Diana's 21st birthday.

Fergie had the right background and the right connections: she shared a flat with Carolyn Beckwith-Smith whose cousin, Anne Beckwith-Smith, is a lady-in-waiting to Diana. Another of Carolyn Beckwith-Smith's cousins is Mrs David Napier, a lady-in-waiting to the Duchess of Kent. And Carolyn herself had a business with Lady Charles Settrington, wife of the Duke of Richmond's photographer grandson: Exclusive Shopping, which aimed to supply unusual goods to tourists and others.

Most interestingly of all Ronald Ferguson's Aunt Jane was married to Sir William Fellowes, long-time land agent at Sandringham. Sir William died, aged 87, in April this year, a month after his wife. His son Robert Fellowes, who is Fergie's cousin, married Diana's elder sister Jane and is an assistant private secretary to the Queen – now number two to Sir William Heseltine – and the couple live at Kensington Palace.

What was more, at one stage Diana even suggested that Fergie should become her lady-in-waiting. But firstly Fergie was considered 'too inexperienced', meaning that she would probably be too conspicuous and not courtierly enough, and secondly Fergie got her job with Richard Burton, which suited her fine. Then, in 1985 when Charles was seeking a new private secretary after a public falling-out with Edward Adeane, some in the court suggested that Ronald Ferguson's name be put forward. Ferguson was actually quite relieved when the job went to 52-year-old baronet Sir John Riddell, director of Crédit Suisse First Boston and married to Bank of England governor Gordon Richardson's daughter Sarah: although Charles needed someone experienced, Ferguson was indispensable as polo manager and frankly he preferred to continue his open-air life at the Guards Polo Club.

The Fergie and Diana connection went deeper. They have similar views on matters of taste in many fields. Extraordinarily, they both received their first kiss from the same man: Diana's first unsung young suitor was James Boughey, good-looking Old Etonian second son of baronet Sir Richard Boughey and a lieutenant in the 9th/12th Lancers. And Fergie's first grown-up kiss was also from a young officer – her cousin James Boughey, son of Sir Richard Boughey and his wife Davina, elder sister of Susie Barrantes, and, like Andrew, a few months younger than Fergie.

Diana and Sarah would quite often meet for a quiet lunch – conveniently halfway between George Street and Kensington Palace – at the light, airy and discreet fourth-floor restaurant of Harvey Nichols in Knightsbridge, a frequent source of Diana's fashion accessories. Or they would go shopping at the General Trading Company in Sloane Street or meet in the West End and go to Fenwicks. If Charles was away, Fergie would go round for supper. And because of Paddy McNally's travelling Fergie was often available for these dates on her own, and because of her troubles with McNally, Diana always had an eye open for any matchmaking opportunities. Diana, like most of Fergie's friends, was concerned to find her a good man who would treat her well.

So it was ironic that Diana, who had been absorbing and learning her role as Princess of Wales at an astonishing rate, did not at an early time spot the full potential in Fergie or regard her as more than a friend, but rather, as time went on, began to prepare herself for having to deal with Andrew's next pretty fancy. For, although Andrew was busy having fun, he did and does deeply respect Charles's opinion and has always brought new girls to Charles for fraternal approval.

Diana was aware that Charles would eventually approve of anyone whom his brother genuinely cared for, however unsuitable – he had even stood up for Koo when she had few allies at the Palace. From time to time Diana herself suggested candidates as suitable dates for Andrew on formal occasions – and that Royal Ascot house party in June of last year was one of those occasions.

Fergie wouldn't be in awe of him and she was among the few who could cope with Andrew's boisterousness. Much has been made of his 'sense of humour', but it is often quite different from that of his brother Charles. Charles's humour is genuinely contemplative, even though he does have musical-hall outbursts – in nervousness before a grand speech announcing: 'As the actress said to the bishop: "This thing is bigger than both of us . . ."' Even now the humour of Andrew could, in general, be described as simpler, even schoolboyish, to the point where it might be thought to be in dubious taste. His chasing of girls in the Bahamas with a live lobster may seem to be funny, but it takes only a moment to realise that for someone sunbathing to open their eyes to the tentacles and claws of a lobster is no laughing matter.

Although his time in the Navy has taught him that gallows humour is often necessary to relieve the tension of the moment, it was hardly well received when he pinched the emerald-skirted bottom of a guest at Sandringham and announced, 'There's Goose Green for you', or when he was drinking his frequent lemonade favourite shortly after the recent American space disaster and remarked that it was as well that Seven-Up was not a new drink looking for a market.

Fergie had a similar sense of humour, simple and jolly, and on that fateful pre-Ascot lunch at Windsor Castle, as Andrew tried to force her to eat the rather phallic chocolate profiteroles and she pretended to resist, she may have had in mind the possibly embarrassing consequences if her liking for Andrew turned into something more.

Even though Diana is now credited with having developed a strength of personality to rival the Queen Mother, she couldn't fix the romance or force it. All that she could do, and did do, was to make it possible.

It was a subtle game. Talking innocently to both sides and seeing how things developed. The most difficult thing for Andrew with his girlfriends had always been privacy and the venues for meetings. But here were the excuses for being somewhere else – he was visiting his brother, she was visiting Diana – that made the whole thing easy. He had found his St James's meeting-place with Koo, but in time it was discovered. There couldn't be that kind of public attention at Kensington Palace.

As far as Diana was concerned, Fergie fitted the bill on a number of counts. Some girls, such as Clare Steel (now Wentworth-Stanley), were so beautiful that they might outshine Diana. Fergie is good-looking, but will never be direct competition for Diana.

If anyone can make a person feel at home it is Fergie; even her stepmother Sue's first recollection of her bears this out. She says: 'It couldn't have been easy for Sarah but right from the start she welcomed me and tried to make me feel part of the family. She is a super person.' So it was with Diana in that year before she married Prince Charles, making her feel one of the family in the polo world. Initially Diana was not keen on the sport, but now she can usually be found with Fergie and friends like Vanessa Llewellyn whenever Charles plays.

Diana is also aware of the mistakes she made when she joined the Family Firm. For instance, over the matter of the David and Elizabeth Emanuel wedding dress: Although it looked splendid when she first appeared in it, had the Emanuels been more experienced they would have put more pellets around the inside of the hem to hold the skirt down so that when she alighted at St Paul's she would not have had to push the skirt out – it was a minor inconvenience, but it was not going to be repeated.

Certainly Diana decided that Fergie should not go to the designers that she favoured. While the best all vied to dress the Princess of Wales, the Princess Andrew would have to find new names. No matter who she chooses to dress her, Fergie can never compete with Diana in the fashion stakes. Diana has an innate sense of style probably inherited from her mother. Fergie has not. She has always thought that there are limited options for a redhead. The hair can only be presented in so many ways and although she will undoubtedly appear in some surprising and glamorous outfits, she will be very pushed to compare with Diana's ethereal looks.

It is Fergie's mother who says that while Jane inherited her mother's figure and her father's calmness, Fergie has her mother's character but not her mother's figure. Diana is a size 10 and has a figure that shows clothes to perfection. Fergie, a couple of inches shorter, is size 14. 'It's my bottom,' she wails. 'What can I do with it?' The answer is: not a lot. The fashion pundits agree on some things – she shouldn't wear trousers, but then Fergie has never worn trousers much. She should keep her weight down; she's been doing that with swims in the Buckingham Palace pool with Diana and with training sessions. She should take time to understand what makes her look good; she will have that time to look good. She is thriving on her relationship with Andrew and is particularly suited to being his wife. But it will be far more difficult to dress Fergie and far easier to make her look frumpy. The best advice she will get is from the girl who has been through it all herself, and who now has a protégée, friend and confidante within the Firm.

There is one irony in the relationship between Fergie and Andrew in that what Diana and Fergie's friends sought for her was a truly fulfilling relationship in which she was an equal partner, not just someone running errands. But, as one friend says: 'She has always walked three paces behind the men in her life. Her father, Kim, Paddy. Now she'll be doing it again.' But this time for the right reasons.

9

Royal Romance

It was at the suggestion of Diana that Sarah was included to make up the numbers for the traditional house party at Windsor Castle. 'What do I do?' she asked her father. His advice was simple: 'Just be yourself, darling.'

To some of their friends, it appeared as though Sarah Ferguson had split up with McNally by the beginning of 1985, but that was not actually the case, for one month before the house party, at the Monaco Grand Prix in May, they had been together at the seafront Mirabeau Hotel on Avenue Princesse-Grace. It was McNally himself who drove her down to Windsor Castle for the Ascot house party. There were a number of young people present and certainly no one, least of all McNally, suspected there was any particular matchmaking going on. And when Fergie first appeared with the royal party, being escorted by Prince Andrew to the unsaddling enclosure at Royal Ascot, she didn't cause a lot of notice for she was immediately recognised with: 'Oh, that's Ronnie Ferguson's daughter' and the media continued its search for putative new romances for Prince Andrew.

No one saw what was, very slowly, unfolding in front of their faces. Fergie had always liked Andrew, but thought of him as liking rather more glamorous types than her, so she wasn't quite sure what to think when, that very week, they shared a goodnight kiss that meant a little more than just goodnight.

They had their first proper evening alone the following week, with time to talk about all kinds of inconsequential matters that seemed so very important at the time. They even spoke about McNally and Fergie was, up to a point, honest about their relationship, saying that they were friends but there was nothing long-term in it.

Andrew had to return to his naval duties for the next two months, and in July Fergie and Paddy McNally headed for Ibiza to stay at the villa belonging to Michael Pearson, while Sean and Rollo McNally visited their grandparents in Monte Carlo. Pearson, eldest son of the immensely wealthy Lord Cowdray, has eschewed the business life to be a bearded playboy around the Mediterranean and he keeps a lavish open house. To the other house guests, Fergie and Paddy still seemed to be very close, and indeed they were. The one difference that McNally noticed throughout their time in the Ibizan breezes was that Fergie hardly seemed at all interested in discussing their relationship and its chances of survival – McNally, with no desire to change the present situation, was a much more loving and considerate companion than usual and they spent a happy time there.

McNally particularly enjoyed the break as the work he had put into All Sport Management, the company he had set up the previous year when he had completed his contract with Philip Morris, was paying off. Based in Geneva, All Sport had become the leading specialist in circuit advertising and through a deal with the Formula One Constructors Association already sold tickets and advertising for Grand Prix races in Belgium, Brazil, Austria, at one of the two French circuits, in Germany and other parts of the world. Their friends and fellow holidaymakers reckoned that the subject of marriage was still a sore one and tried not to mention the word.

But after the Ibiza holiday the break-ups of the two seemed to become more frequent. One girlfriend was present when Fergie had walked out on McNally at Drones, the smart Pont Street hamburger restaurant owned by film producer David Niven Jr and Nicky Kerman, the Scott's restaurateur who is a good friend of McNally's chalet co-owner, David Elias.

In September 1985 Sarah, once again in tears over McNally's perpetual flirtations, was telling Paddy that it would be a good idea if they didn't see each other. Meanwhile Andrew, who already had some media experience from appearing on American television with David Frost, was interviewed by Sue MacGregor for Radio 4's *Woman's Hour* and gave nothing away on his current romantic status. When asked if he was looking for a wife who knew the ropes or someone who would make a good Navy wife, he said: 'The honest answer is that I don't know what I'm looking for yet, simply because I haven't had any chance to think about it.' And on his brother Charles's view that about thirty was the right age to marry, he replied: 'It'll happen and if it happens who knows when it is going to happen? I know that if I do find somebody, then it is going to come like a lightning bolt and you're going to know it there and then.' And he added, '*If* is a very big word.'

Another incident that drew Andrew and Fergie closer together was the excitement over the birth of Eliza, the fifth Ferguson child and Sarah's second half-sister, on 9 October. Prince Charles had agreed to be a godfather to the little girl, and as Fergie said: 'We'll almost be related.'

There was hardly a definite break-up point in the relationship between Fergie and McNally, but in October at the Italian Grand Prix at Imola the relationship did seem to come to a head. McNally did not want any commitment (on his side anyway) and if Fergie did, she must look elsewhere. It was as simple as that. Yet Fergie seemed remarkably cheerful about it all, and Paddy reckoned that, as on previous occasions, in time she would be back. It was all quite amicable and it hardly occurred to him that there was someone else.

Likewise there was hardly a definite moment when Fergie knew that her relationship with Andrew, which had been growing over the summer and early autumn, was more than just another of his flings, although she did tell him: 'I don't just want to be another one of Andy's women.' But there was a slow realisation in her mind that she liked Andrew, found him attractive and, although she wasn't sure whether this was true love, that if she played her cards right she could become Prince Andrew's bride.

She was certainly happier and more cheeful than usual and several of her friends remarked on it. 'Love,' she told one inquirer, blithely. But she wouldn't be drawn and most thought she was talking of McNally. She was also extremely busy. At work things were hectic because of the scale of Richard Burton's latest project, *The Palace of Westminster*, an illustrated history of the treasures of the Lords and the Commons, with text by Sir Robert Cooke, Labour MP for Edinburgh Central, which needed organisation of photographs, printers, text and researchers that would often require her to stay late at the office and take papers and proofs home with her.

There was hardly time to think about another problem on her horizons: for Carolyn Beckwith-Smith, then 30, and her 24-year-old Old Etonian boyfriend Harry Cotterell, two years younger than Fergie, seemed on the point of making a decision about their future. If, as Carolyn thought, they did get married then Fergie would have to find somewhere else to live.

Bouquets of roses began to arrive at Fergie's flat, accompanied by sealed notes signed with an 'A', as Andrew and Fergie's pleasure in each other's company grew, and it seemed to Fergie that this might be more than another Andrew fling.

Press interest in Andrew had not waned, it was just that the newsmen were waiting to see what he would get up to next. Andrew, who says of his own photographic efforts: 'My family always cringe when they hear the sound of a motor-drive camera, even if it is mine', did not want to disappoint them. When he went with Hugh Wooldridge to see Wooldridge's production of *Split Second* at the Lyric Theatre, Hammersmith – a fringe theatre production about a black New York policeman who shoots a white policeman, Andrew's first experience of the Fringe and very different from his normal entertainment – there was a new girl on his arm. The flash bulbs went off all over town when she was seen leaving the Palace with him. Andrew kept his head down in time-honoured tradition, but this time he had succeeded in laying a false trail. Nobody recognised Wooldridge's two production assistants, Clare Fynn and Mandy Gough, so another 'romance' was born. Early next morning Andrew had a call from Fergie, teasingly asking if he had had a good time at the theatre. 'Andrew's new girlfriend is rather pretty, isn't she?' she even asked one colleague that day.

HMS *Brazen* was in Devonport from 18 December to 20 January, which allowed the couple plenty of opportunity for clandestine meetings, well away from the prying eyes of the press. There were more suppers at Clapham, the Jaguar parked around the corner, more meetings at Buckingham Palace, with just one discreet footman bringing a light supper before leaving them alone.

Sometimes they managed to go away together for the weekend, staying with trusted friends such as Gordonstoun schoolfriends of Andrew, Charlotte Eden, now married to Lord McGowan's farmer son Mungo and living on the 850-acre family estate in Braunston, Northampton, the Roxburghes (Andrew would sometimes call into the Roxburghe-owned Sunlaws Hotel for an evening drink to let folk know he was 'on his own') and others.

On Christmas Eve, a Tuesday and a normal working day for many, customers at Garrard's, otherwise known as the Goldsmiths and Silversmiths Company and Crown Jewellers, were surprised to see Andrew walk through the front door on Regent Street. The floorwalker, whose job it is to direct customers to the right department, could hardly believe his eyes. 'Your Royal Highness,' he announced grandly, 'I will tell Mr Somers (the managing director and crown jeweller) that you are here.' The few Americans and others doing their last-minute Christmas shopping started round at the pronouncement. But Andrew had a new devil-may-care attitude towards his appearances and some last-minute shopping to do before Christmas which he reckoned it would be quicker to do himself. He didn't quite know what he wanted. He specified that he wanted to buy some jewellery as a present for someone. He found a Russian wedding-ring of three different golds that exactly suited his purpose.

Fergie had been busy, too. It was later that afternoon that her BMW had swept through the gates of Buckingham Palace and she went up to Andrew's apartment to deliver her presents.

What neither of them realised was that they were not the only ones who had been busy that day. At Windsor Castle the family were preparing for their traditional Christmas Eve black tie dinner – presents are exchanged afterwards and on Christmas Day after a traditional lunch the family fend for themselves and have cold food. There were a succession of informal discussions between the Queen, Prince Philip, the Queen Mother and finally Prince Charles – almost a major shareholders' meeting in the Family Firm. There was only one major subject on the agenda: Andrew and Sarah.

What did they all think? There had been a certain amount of discreet canvassing among the court and of course there was no reason to suggest that Prince Andrew would ever become king. On the other hand, there was equally no point in upsetting the millions of supporters of the royal family by taking a hasty or rash decision. Did they think Sarah was right for Andrew?

Prince Philip was a keen supporter of Sarah. He had always liked Ferguson and thought him a good sort, and his daughter was certainly a lively girl. What was more, he said, and this eventually became the most important factor, there was no doubt that Sarah Ferguson was the first girlfriend Andrew had produced who was actually suitable. Here was a well-bred, nice, working girl. Attractive enough and sensible enough to let Andrew get on with his life while she got on with hers.

The negative aspect was the stories that had been in the press about her two former lovers. They had both been offered large sums to 'tell all', but both were too well-brought-up to blab and, more importantly, well enough off not to need the money bribes. Frankly, even if they had been interested in money they were better off in the long term by staying in with Fergie than they could possibly be by taking any payment. Discreet inquiries had been made by the Palace. Smith-Bingham, after a spell working for Gor-Tex skisuits' Event outlet, was now married to Fiona Macdonald-Buchanan, had a baby daughter, Marina, and had set up his own Fulham-based operation importing the American Powderhorn skiwear. McNally's All Sport was thriving and, intriguingly, at his chalet McNally was now surrounded by photographs of Fergie while starting a romance with Becky Few-Brown who had worked for him as a chalet girl in Fergie's time.

The Queen Mother was a Fergie supporter on this. 'Of course an attractive girl of twenty-six will have had previous boyfriends,' she said, matter-of-factly. 'I think she'll be ideal for him.'

It was Charles, previously briefed by Diana, who made the final comment. 'Well, all I can say is that I like Sarah very much. She's a good sort and frankly I think she'd be a great asset to Andrew and to the rest of us – that is, of course, if she'll have him!'

A ploy was decided. None of them would say anything unless Andrew brought up the subject, but they would do whatever they could to help – Diana needed no second bidding – and although Andrew had already invited Sarah up to Sandringham for the New Year celebrations, the Queen would herself make it a personal invitation.

And so Andrew arrived that evening to a particularly happy family gathering.

At Dummer Down House, talking to his daughter, Ronnie Ferguson reckoned that at last she had found the relationship she wanted. How it would end, time alone would tell, but it seemed to be reaching that point of intensity where the couple would either have to get engaged or decide to split up. While the children romped on

Christmas morning, Fergie and Andrew spoke on the phone and it was then that they both realised that they knew their own minds. The Russian wedding-ring, which just fitted the little finger of her right hand, was to her mind, perfection. But Fergie knew that now she had to face her most difficult time, the final testing. For there was no mistaking that to keep her man now, Sarah had to be discreet, careful and even, possibly, clever.

10

Felicitas Crescit

It was on 1 January 1986, when Fergie went to spend five days at Sandringham as the personal guest of the Queen, that the press and television world knew that there really was something happening. This was the first time since Koo that any girlfriend of Andrew had received a personal invitation from her. They were very happy days for both of them and, away from the crowds, Fergie and Andrew spent long hours together.

By now the press was hot on the heels of the unfortunate Ferguson family and it was a trying time at Dummer Down House. For Major Ferguson it was particularly difficult. On top of what seemed like the minor problems of the world's media on his doorstep and the christening he was organising for Eliza, his daughter Jane was, yet again, expecting a baby – and after having suffered two recent miscarriages, at six months and eight months, everyone was understandably nervous.

'I didn't want it to get out of hand,' says Major Ferguson. 'That was a very nervous week. Frankly anything else was rather pushed into the background until we knew about Jane.'

The Major would have been even more nervous if he had realised what was going on at Sandringham. For on New Year's Eve Andrew, in the traditionally awkward way of a young man, summoned up the courage to suggest to Fergie that they should get married. As delighted as she was by the offer, Fergie didn't lose her head. 'That's a lovely idea,' she said. 'But do you think we're ready for that? Aren't you

happy as we are? And anyway you have to ask me properly
. . .' She wouldn't have taken much persuading, but
Andrew, who had spent hours and days agonising up to that
point, didn't see that. He wasn't sure where this left him.
She hadn't said Yes, and she hadn't said No. She hadn't
even said Maybe.

They continued their relaxed and happy days. Every
other member of the family knew they would get engaged,
but they didn't. This would, Diana thought, obviously take
a bit more time.

On 6 January Andrew rejoined HMS *Brazen* and Fergie
returned to Clapham. Fergie was busy, but there were
many hours spent on the phone to Diana, and meetings for
lunch at the restaurant on the top floor of Harvey Nichols –
Diana was one of the very few people she could trust. And
it was Diana who gave her some advice: for heaven's sake
start looking around at dress designers right away. Diana
had originally thought of using Bill Pashley, a Battersea-
based dress designer and maker popular among Diana's
friends, to make the royal wedding gown. She'd been put
off this by the courtiers on the grounds that he was a
one-man operation, to whom anything could happen. An
alternative list was drawn up and David and Elizabeth
Emanuel were chosen. Although just out of the Royal
College of Art, they had successfully set up their business
with the help of Elizabeth's retired supermarket tycoon
father. So Diana's advice was: start looking now, don't be
caught out – which is exactly what Fergie did.

There had been some further excitement in Lavender
Gardens as Carolyn and Harry Cotterell had finally
announced their engagement. They would marry in July
and they would move to Hereford where Harry would help
his father, baronet Sir John Cotterell, run the family estate.
There was plenty of celebration, toasts in champagne and
also plenty of quizzing of Fergie, her friends saying archly:
'You'll be next, Fergie.' She tried to play it cool, but
couldn't hide her happiness.

'Where are you going to live?' asked more than one pal.

Fergie just laughed. 'I'll find somewhere,' she said. 'I've already got my eye on one or two places.' 'Places or palaces?' went the story among her friends.

But Fergie followed Diana's advice about being well prepared. In January she visited the Fulham terrace home of dressmaker Lindka Cierach, a former *Vogue* secretary who had studied at the London College of Fashion, trained with Valentino and Yuki, and had set up in business for herself. Fergie went with Carolyn, who had chosen Lindka to make her wedding dress, and Fergie talked to her about ideas that might possibly work 'for someone like me' and that 'would hide a big bottom'.

Lindka was not entirely unknown for she had been nominated 'hottest society dressmaker of the year' in *Tatler* magazine and had made dresses for the Duchess of Westminster, the Queen of Greece and the Duchess of Kent as well as some stunning wedding dresses, such as the mink-trimmed gown for Lady Rose Cecil, the dress with an eighteen-foot train for Charlotte Monckton, and a 'fairy-tale' gown for Pandora Stevens, daughter of one-time newspaperman turned Rector of the Royal College of Art, Jocelyn Stevens. Lindka was a dressmaker rather than a dress designer and the finish on her gowns was fantastic. Fergie hadn't visited her before purely because she hadn't been able to afford it, for Lindka's creations, often with extraordinarily intricate beadwork, cost upwards of £2,000 and were out of Fergie's league.

It still was a daydream, but as Fergie said: 'You never know when you might need it . . .'

By now the pressure was building up, and the Queen was happy to help relieve it by suggesting that, if they had nowhere to go, Fergie should stay the weekend of 11 and 12 January at the Palace.

By 16 January the press had tracked down Susie Barrantes in Miami, who – according to some newspapers – gave away the fact that her daughter was in love. In fact, this was just a very imaginative interpretation of the lack of comment that Susie gave. In her regular outfit of jeans and shirt (the newsman who asked her for a photograph of herself in a dress were unlucky – she couldn't find one) and surrounded by her three Irish wolfhounds, three Basset hounds, Labrador and Jack Russell terrier, Susie was ever friendly, ever polite, and genuinely happy that Sarah had found her own happiness for whatever reason. Unwittingly she said too much and sooner or later the journalists picked on something that they could write as a confirmation of the match. Her only words on the subject were in answer to the question, 'Is Fergie in love with Prince Andrew?' Susie merely shrugged and said: 'How can I say?' What the newspapers did fail to discover was the strain there was on the marriage of the present Susan Ferguson. In fact, but for the turn of events, they might well have split because of Ferguson's waywardness.

On 18 and 19 January, at the invitation of the Queen, Fergie was again at Sandringham to be reunited with the prince. Then Andrew rejoined HMS *Brazen* on 20 January and sailed for Gothenburg, to return on 4 February for four days.

At Dummer there was very happy news. For in Australia, Jane had given birth to a beautiful, and perfect, baby girl and the telephone lines between Australia and Argentina and England were buzzing. At El Pucarà the strain was as great as anywhere, for the only shadow on the lives of Hector and Susie was the fact that they could not have any children of their own.

For the last weekend in January Fergie went to Highgrove to stay with Charles and Diana, the following weekend they came to Hampshire, for the christening of Fergie's baby sister, Eliza, at the parish church of St Michael, North Waltham – with Charles as a godfather and tea afterwards at Dummer Down House. Andrew had been invited but couldn't come as he was at sea.

Ferguson had hoped to have the christening at Dummer's All Saints Church – one of the ten prettiest in England, John Betjeman had called it – but the vicar, the Rev. Tom Kime, has a rule that he only performs

christenings as part of the Sunday morning service and
Ferguson failed to persuade him to make an exception; he
made no mention of Charles and Diana's presence, but
felt that a public ceremony would be unwise with them
present.

Three days later, on 5 February, Fergie accompanied
Charles and Diana and three-and-a-half-year-old William
on a visit to HMS *Brazen*, in port for a four-day goodwill
visit, and Diana instructed her, none too silently: 'Keep
smiling, for goodness sake.' They returned in the evening
without William for a party on board.

Diana had already suggested a daring stroke: that Fergie
should join her and Charles on their traditional Klosters
skiing holiday. If she wanted to know whether she could
stand up to being in the public eye, this would be as good a
test as any. The press were beside themselves when, on 6
February, Fergie, with a Buckingham Palace aide by her
side and wearing a glamorous fur hat ring with a tail – a kind
of topless Davy Crockett affair – turned up in Klosters with
Charles and Diana for an official photocall. Charles and
Diana had taken to holding these photocalls in the hope
that thereafter they would be left alone by the media. The
attention was a strain but Diana turned to Fergie, smiled
and again instructed her, through smiling lips, to 'keep
smiling'. And they did keep smiling, the next day turning
out in identical powder-blue ski-suits and matching white
fur hatbands, the better to confuse any pursuing photographers – although frankly, for the paparazzo crew, this
time Fergie was as good a catch as Diana.

It was a relaxed week, but when Fergie returned to
London on St Valentine's Day there was a near riot of
photographers and television cameramen at Heathrow
who clambered over luggage carousels and the bonnet of
her car to take her photograph. Police had to elbow a way
clear for her to get into the car. Although she appeared
calm, she didn't say anything and when the car wouldn't
start, she was quickly taken away by police until it could be
fixed. Fergie told a friend that evening: 'I don't know why

they do that – they must have hundreds of photographs of me already.'

After a weekend staying with her father, she was back at work on the Monday, protesting: 'I'm just a normal working girl. I do a full five-day week.' But her trips to her Hanover Square office by 9 a.m. each morning were increasingly dogged by pressmen. And her father was pressed into making a comment on matters. He was, quite rightly, noncommittal: 'I certainly wouldn't assume anything in a boy and girl relationship. I am close to my daughter and she'll tell me what I need to know when there's anything to tell. I don't pry. It's a cliché to say "they are just good friends". They have a normal boy-girl relationship.'

Fergie exchanged politenesses with the reporters, in marked contrast to the awkwardness shown by Diana when she was being courted by Charles. In denying that she had been on any secret assignations she would only say: 'I'm working for a graphic design company. I'm busy and haven't the time to gad around the country.'

Charles flew out to America on the 17 February for a five-day trip to Texas, celebrating its 150th anniversary, which meant there was more time for Diana and Fergie to plot the future.

Andrew spent his 26th birthday on 19 February below decks on HMS *Brazen* at Devonport preparing the paperwork for the debriefing following the frigate's participation in Exercise Western Chance in the South Western Approaches. On the Thursday *Brazen* set sail for her adopted port of Sunderland.

On the morning of Friday 21 February, Fergie spent over an hour with senior stylist Michael at his Albemarle Street salon, *Michaeljohn* (she had recently swopped from Leonard), where she had her hair lightly cut, washed and dried at a cost of £23.50, along with a £5.75 manicure. She was whisked behind a makeshift screen arrangement in the basement, rather in the way that the Duchess of Kent and other notables are when they visit the salon.

However, an Australian girl having the same treatment recognised Fergie leaving and decided that she would make discreet inquiries, thinking that at least Fergie would confide in her hairdresser, even if she didn't in her father and couldn't in her mother. But all she managed to find out was that Fergie, discreet as ever, had not even discussed her love life with Michael, although one of the staff did say: 'She always seems so happy and cheerful – maybe she's even more so at the moment, but it's hard to know.'

And Fergie continued to go off on her travels. When Andrew was once more on land on 22 February, she flew up to Scotland to stay with the Duke and Duchess of Roxburghe, who had always remained among Andrew's very few close and trusted friends. The Roxburghe's magnificent nineteenth-century palace, Floors Castle, has over 130 rooms and plenty of places for privacy, as the prince had discovered when he had taken earlier girlfriends, including Koo, to stay there. The duke, who is five years older than Andrew, is hugely wealthy and has business interests throughout the world, and the duchess is the younger sister of Leonora (estranged wife of photographer earl Patrick Lichfield) and of Gerald, the Duke of Westminster. Their butler John Hudson, who previously worked for Princess Anne, is the ultimate in discretion and ensured peace for the princely presence, even with bodyguard Geoffrey Padgham and the Kelso police in the background.

There is only one thing that is not perfect about Floors Castle, as one guest reports: 'The four-poster beds are too high off the ground.'

But for Andrew and Fergie the place was ideal for a couple as passionate as they were. They could be with each other behind closed doors and, even when Guy and Jane Roxburghe were around, they couldn't resist touching each other or holding hands. And Andrew did something quite unexpected. Making up for his Sandringham effort, in an over-formal way he dropped on both knees and said: 'Miss Ferguson, will you marry me?'

For a moment Fergie was caught off-guard but she managed to enter into the spirit of things. 'Certainly, sir, I will.'
But, serious for a moment, she told him: 'If you wake up
and change your mind in the morning, I'll quite understand.'

'No, no,' he averred. 'I really did mean it.'

And agreeing that they should keep their secret to
themselves until Andrew had spoken to Fergie's father and
the Queen, they went to meet Guy and Jane Roxburghe.
'Could we have a bottle of champagne, please?' asked
Andrew, and Hudson was sent off to get a bottle of the
finest champagne from the cellar.

Diana invited Fergie to spend the night of 3 March at
Kensington Palace so that the couple could meet in peace,
and by 4 March Andrew was back at his Buckingham
Palace quarters for one week on shore leave. There were
three things that Andrew had on his list of priorities: he
must get Fergie a ring, he must speak to his mother and he
must speak to her father. He was not quite sure how to go
about the tasks, but he started by calling a whole selection
of royal jewellers to the palace with a selection of their
rings. Collingwood, much favoured by Diana, Asprey's in
Bond Street and Garrard, the crown jewellers, all brought
trays of rings to his rooms – not actually trays, but a handful
of rings, wrapped and pushed casually in the pocket. The
couple had already decided that they would go for a ruby,
and after examination of all the offerings, although Fergie
found several rings she liked Andrew said that he really
didn't feel that any of them were of the quality he wanted
for her. The one they liked best was from Collingwood, but
he returned to Garrard's, the crown jewellers who had
made the engagement rings for Diana and Princess Anne,
to see if they could produce a similar ring in a larger size.
Prince Andrew assisted with the drawings of what he
wanted and Fergie had already found her size, so it was left
to the workrooms of Garrard, high above the Regent Street
traffic, to fashion the large oval ruby set in a ring of drop
diamonds – they decided on ten – on a band of white gold.

Amazingly, it was completed in just one week, and the arrangement was that it would be kept in the safe at Garrard's meanwhile. Despite those that said otherwise, Fergie did not keep the ring on a chain around her neck – she didn't trust herself, and it was only delivered to Prince Andrew on the morning of the engagement announcement. That was when she wore it for the very first time.

On the night of Tuesday 11 March they appeared together at a public event for the first time when they went off to see the Royal Ballet in the avant-garde programme of *Frankenstein, the Modern Prometheus* at the Royal Opera House in Covent Garden. The manager was given only a few hours' notice of the prince's presence and it was stressed that it was essentially a private visit. Arriving in the prince's Jaguar, the photographers got their first glimpse of the couple together, although they craftily left in different directions from the Opera House afterwards. But the speculation about them increased with the imminent return of the Queen from Australia.

Major Ferguson had the feeling that something was up, and, ever the consummate public relations man, had the situation well in hand. To avoid a rush of press interest, he took the precaution of giving some interviews or, more accurately, briefings to some newspapers about Fergie on the strict understanding that they would not be used 'until there is some sort of announcement'. And he contacted Fergie's old school, Hurst Lodge, asking them not to give out any information 'until there was some sort of announcement'.

On Saturday 15 March Andrew and Fergie went to Windsor for Andrew to talk to the Queen.

In most circumstances the prospective bridegroom would ask the bride's father first, but with the royal family things are different. Without Ronald Ferguson's agreement, they could have still gone ahead and done what they wished. Without the Queen's approval there could be no marriage. There was little chance of her saying no but, as the couple drove along the M4 from London, there was no more nervous and apprehensive pair in the country.

While Fergie stayed in her room, Andrew had his interview with the Queen – 'there's something I wanted to have
a word with you about, Mother'. She already knew what he
was going to say and she was delighted when he said it.

Philip, pointed out that Andrew had yet to ask her
father. 'What if he says no?' mused Philip. 'I suppose you
can always send the ring back.' 'I'm sure that he'll be all
right,' Fergie said, 'and anyway we can always get married
without his permission.' There was much hilarity and
happiness as more champagne was drunk to Fergie joining
the Family Firm.

On the Sunday Fergie had lunch with the Queen at
Windsor Castle while Prince Andrew was on official duties
at the All England Badminton Championships at Wemb-
ley. He just smiled in noncommittal style at any mention of
marriage. That afternoon Fergie travelled to Dummer and
drove her BMW past the waiting reporters and up the drive
with its notice 'Slow – Children and horses'. How did the
meeting at Windsor go? Fergie, straight-faced, said: 'That
would be telling, wouldn't it?' But the reporters' attention
was distracted enough for them not to notice the green
Jaguar that pulled up through the farm entrance to the back
of the main house.

Andrew was surprised by how nervous he was as he
formally asked Ferguson for the hand of his daughter.
Afterwards, Ferguson admitted that he couldn't say anything immediately, such was his happiness, but just shook
Andrew's hand with a firm and enthusiastic grip.

Andrew drove back to London, evading the still-waiting
reporters – as a military man he has scant regard for the
problems of evading the newspaper 'enemy' – while Fergie
spent the night at Dummer and her father made a quick
phone call to Australia – nine hours ahead of British time –
to tell Jane the good news and to say that he was all set to
see her that Friday. Jane let out a yelp of joy. She had been
kept aware of developments, but when the engagement
was official it was still a surprise. The conversation was
essentially slightly coded, and anyone listening in would

have only thought that they were discussing her father's trip. Jane says: 'News of the engagement was a bit of a surprise, but when we received *that* phone call to say it was official, we were thrilled.'

Fergie drove up to London early on Monday morning, arriving for work as usual – with one conspicuous difference; today she had two policemen in uniform and a plainclothes man to take her through the press cordon outside her office. Although this had happened once before, after she returned from her skiing holiday in Klosters, to the reporters it confirmed without doubt that the engagement was on and they pestered her all the way. But now she was extra-confident at dealing with them. 'I'm not saying anything,' she said. 'But it is a lovely day, isn't it?' And she did rather give the game away by posing extra-willingly for the photographers.

That morning at a cabinet meeting at 10 Downing Street Margaret Thatcher announced that the Queen had told her that her son Andrew was to marry Sarah Ferguson. But the engagement would not be officially announced until Wednesday to avoid overshadowing Tuesday's Budget – after all, affairs of state still had to come first.

Because of the media attention, the Queen had suggested that it would be best if Fergie moved into Buckingham Palace under royal protection. When the Queen makes a suggestion, the wise carry out that suggestion, and on Tuesday 18 March Fergie, with the help of Sue ('This is my wicked stepmother,' as Fergie introduced her to inquiring newsmen), packed her things at Lavender Gardens for the last time.

On the morning of Wednesday 19 March the announcement was made at Buckingham Palace: 'It is with great pleasure that the Queen and Prince Philip announce the betrothal of their beloved son, Prince Andrew, to Miss Sarah Ferguson, daughter of Major Ronald Ferguson and Mrs Hector Barrantes.'

The excitement was such at the Palace that the notice was dated wrongly – 19 February, Prince Andrew's birthday –

and posted at 10.00, one hour earlier than the announcement was expected. Hordes of press and TV folk flocked around. Official engagement pictures of the couple were released – they'd been taken at the weekend by Prince Andrew himself with a delayed-action exposure and with the Queen and Prince Philip looking on.

It was arranged that Andrew and Fergie would give a television interview for release to the world. They sat side by side on a sofa in his study, made all the more nervous and apprehensive by the fact that the Queen, who was enjoying herself hugely, was sitting in on the filming. Fergie proudly showed off her ruby-and-ten-teardrop diamond ring. 'It had to be something red. I wanted a ruby – well, I didn't want a ruby, I'm very lucky to have it.' Suddenly realising what she was saying, she was slightly flustered, but Andrew saved her: 'We came to the conclusion that red was probably the best colour for Sarah.'

Under Fergie's guidance – Andrew felt that here was a girl who could sort out any tricky questions – they faced up to it with banter and good humour. She said that she liked his 'wit, charm and sense of good humour': in the same spirit he added that he liked 'her red hair'. Fergie admitted it had been a strain to keep the engagement secret 'but only because I wanted everyone to share my happiness'.

Asked how he felt, Andrew replied: 'Over the moon. Correction. We're both over the moon and will be even more so when this is over.'

Fergie said: 'We are a good team. We are good friends. I am going to enjoy it immensely. I think I will cope with the help of Andrew.' Andrew added: 'I think we have discovered in the last nine months that we can work together.' Fergie said that she hoped to continue working: 'I enjoy my work enormously. When Andrew is away I will work harder than when he is here.' Andrew nodded in agreement: 'Sarah is her own boss and she can make her own schedule to suit herself.'

Of his future, he said: 'I will be maintaining my naval career as it is at the moment. It is up to Sarah to put up with

that and I think she will be a remarkable wife if she can . . .
I have absolutely no plans to change the course of my life
because I am to be married. And in any case Sarah has told
me in no uncertain terms not to change my plans, at least
for the foreseeable future.'

Of the thunderbolt he had forecast, Andrew said, 'I am
at a loss really to say . . . I don't think Sarah is a thunderbolt as I expected.' And Fergie giggled: 'Nor am I streak of
lightning . . . nor is he.' Yes, she was looking for a dress,
and she turned inquiringly to Andrew. 'Yes, thank you, I
already have my dress,' Andrew said.

They walked out on to the back terrace of the Palace and
across the somewhat rain-sodden lawn and, encouraged by
the cameramen, they kissed. After all it had been Andrew
who had cajoled Charles and Diana into the now famous
public post-wedding kiss on the Palace balcony. 'Let's
make it a smacker,' said Fergie, kissing him on the lips. But
Andrew looked a bit awkward and said: 'Once is enough.'

Even allowing for some nervousness in front of the
television cameras, the message that came across in that
interview was clear: Here was no dewy-eyed young couple,
blinded by romantic love. Andrew had conformed to the
training of his formative years and chosen as his wife a
suitable business partner for the Family Firm.

At Heathrow Airport Major Ferguson watched the
events on a television screen as he waited to catch his flight
to Australia. He was bursting with happiness and pride. 'I
am extremely proud of the way she has, over the past three
or four months, coped with the problems presented by
constant media attention. She has handled it superbly . . .
Obviously I am biased but she has handled herself extremely well under conditions often amounting to extreme pro-
vocation.'

And to queries as to how she would cope with being a
member of the royal family, he said that her behaviour so
far had given a pretty good indication that she would cope
quite well. 'She is a very sweet girl, a very kind girl. With a
great deal of common sense. She attempts to enjoy life to

its full. She unquestionably tries to get the maximum out of life in the shortest possible time.'

His experience of dealing with the media showed through. 'I have managed to live a hundred per cent normal life while the speculation has been going on. The pressure has been on Sarah, not me, and she has coped marvellously.' And he went on record for the first time on the subject of Prince Andrew: 'I think he is a very fine person. We all know he's a professional helicopter pilot and I admire anybody who is a professional at their job.'

Unsurprisingly, Prince Charles, at the private viewing of an exhibition of watercolours (including two of his own) at the Mall Gallery, said: 'I couldn't be more delighted. She is wonderful.'

The engagement was reported around the world, particularly in the Argentinian press where, despite, or maybe because of, the troubles and the republicanism of the country, people have a deep fascination for all things English and, particularly, all things royal. *Flash* reported, '*El Principito se casa con la hijastra de voluntario Argentino en guerra de Malvinas*' – 'the princeling marries the stepdaughter of an Argentinian volunteer in the Malvinas War', and *Gente* reported, '*Toda Europa habla de ella*' – 'all Europe is talking of her' – and enthused about '*Sarah y Andy Randy (como llaman sus familiares al principe Andres)*' – 'Sarah and Andy Randy (as Prince Andrew is called by those close to him)'.

Koo Stark, who had been watching the television interview at her home, said, as one would expect: 'It's wonderful news. I wish them both the greatest happiness.'

It was six days later, on 25 March, that further speculation about the marriage was ended with the announcement that they would be married by the Archbishop of Canterbury at Westminster Abbey on Wednesday 23 July.

There were those who were none too happy with the relative speed – in royal terms – of the wedding. Many courtiers had already booked their summer holidays and had to change dates, the BBC had to reorganise their outside broadcast camera schedules to make sufficient cameras available and there were plenty of anguished cries in Fleet Street as journalists on the royal beat had to pacify irate wives and persuade them to alter their plans. On HMS *Brazen*, whom Andrew had rung early in the morning that day, there were many toasts in the Officers' Mess and among the men, although there was some unhappiness that they were due to be in the Middle East on 23 July so couldn't make a personal guard of honour. Lieutenant Commander Angus Sinclair said: 'It's a shame we won't be a bit nearer but we'll be thinking of them.'

In Switzerland the newspaper *Tribune de Genève* boasted, '*La fiancée d'Andrew est un peu Genevoise*', basing this assertion on the fact that BCK Graphic Arts SA have their headquarters in Geneva. And the London Tourist Board's June Primmer said: 'It is worth millions to us.'

Fergie's father, who had organised things so well and would not be around to handle Fergie's promotion as he was off to Australia, made an informal statement from Heathrow: 'I'm absolutely thrilled. I am very happy for Sarah and I think Prince Andrew will make a marvellous son-in-law.'

On behalf of the red-headed population, Jane Asher said: 'I would like to express our thanks to Prince Andrew for having the good taste to pick such an excellent example of our breed. At last the world will recognise that, far from being the bad-tempered, pasty-faced carrot-heads so rudely referred to, we are delicate, ethereal, Titian-tressed princesses who must be treated with the respect we deserve. And anyone who says different had better *bloody well watch out*!'

Fergie herself positively glowed, more aware each day of the details of her Image. One day she'd be seen in a Daniel Hechter sweater, the next in an Alistair Blair outfit, carrying a Louis Vuitton overnight bag and flashing *that* ring.

The genealogists brought out their charts and declared that Sarah, through the family of the Duke of Buccleuch, was related to Charles II, and so could be said to be far more royal than Prince Andrew with all his German antecedents.

In Buenos Aires Susie Barrantes was ecstatic. Sarah had some experience of life she said, so there would be little chance of her making the mistakes her mother had made. What was more, on the day of the engagement you could see clearly that Sarah was wearing the heart-shaped diamond studs that Susie had given her. Her mother had to wipe a tear away as she said: 'The important thing to me is that Sarah is so happy. She and Prince Andrew are engaged and that is all that really matters. And I hope that they will be as happy as Hector and I have been.

'She will be a wonderful princess because now she is totally happy. And when you're happy, you've always got more to give, not only to your partner but to everyone else as well. That's something Hector taught me.

'We are thrilled about the engagement. I love Sarah very much. She is a very popular young woman and she has tremendous strength.'

Not all commentators were quite as enthusiastic. There was a feeling that Sarah had 'been around' and that she had 'a past'. There was even the reaction from a long-serving staff member of one gentlemen's club that 'once a girl's started, she can't stop'. The fact that Andrew had a past, too, was dismissed with a shrug and the brief comment 'he is a man'.

The two boyfriends in Fergie's life kept a suitable silence. Smith-Bingham, now married with a child, said nothing. Nor, despite offers of increased sums of money, did McNally, except to comment: 'Any man would be lucky to go out with her – let alone marry her. She is a marvellous lady – an outstanding woman. Any task she took on she'd be more than mistress of.' And one of the McNally crowd said: 'I have been pleasantly surprised by Paddy. He has behaved very honourably.' It didn't take long before photographs of McNally and Fergie on holiday at Michael Pearson's house in Ibiza the previous year surfaced in the French magazine *Paris Match*. One photograph even surfaced featuring a girl naked in a bath, but McNally's friend Nigel Pollitzer announced: 'That's not Fergie, that's my girlfriend in the bath.'

The weekend after the engagement there was only one place for the happy, and relieved, couple: Floors Castle in Scotland, where they would be undisturbed, quiet, and where they knew they would be among friends. Guy and Jane Roxburghe had been delighted at the official announcement and were more than happy to let the couple lead their own life. As before, the couple were put into adjoining four-poster guest suites. As before, staff were given instructions not to disturb them.

All kinds of formalities had to be gone through. For instance, as Peter Spurrier, Portcullis Pursuivant at the Royal College of Arms, said: 'It is appropriate for a person marrying into the royal family to have their own heraldic identity.' It is interesting in this connection that both Princess Anne and Prince Andrew married non-armigerous people – that is, not bearing arms. A grant of arms was made to Mark Phillips's father Peter, but for Fergie it would be made directly to her. So she went for consultations with the Garter King of Arms, the Queen approved the designs, and on 14 April the arms were granted – a bee on a thistle with the motto 'Ex Adversis Felicitas Crescit' (Through adversity happiness grows) on the triangular lozenge on which all female arms appear. It was suggested at the time that the significance of the bee on the thistle was that Fergie was always so busy, which is not the case at all. The real reason for the arms was that the Fergusons have a number of pieces of old family silver engraved with a crest incorporating a bee on a thistle. Not even Major Ferguson or his mother knew where that crest had come from. In fact, it belonged to the family of John Maguennis of Burt House in County Donegal (some of the Guinness family claim the same root), who, in 1860, took the name of his wealthy maternal uncle, Sir Andrew Ferguson, whose son Sir Robert had died without heirs. The *General Armoury*, often considered a bit slapdash, was probably requested, in the the middle of the nineteenth century, to find a suitable crest for some Ferguson silver. That crest is now raised to full armorial status.

Andrew's life also underwent changes. He had said farewell to HMS *Brazen* after two years as her helicopter pilot with much parting merriment. On his last tour of inspection, the ten Royal Marines on board provided some welcome light relief. One stopped the prince, saluted smartly and announced: 'Royal Marines' Mess ready for inspection, sir.' The prince stepped into a large darkened cabin, the lights were suddenly switched on and the Marines all sprang to attention. But the men, including Falklands and Ulster veterans, were hardly dressed in a correct manner, for they wore an extraordinary selection of shortie nighties, see-through bodices, suspender belts and stockings. 'We really set him up good and proper.' Andrew rose to the occasion and solemnly went down the line commenting on details: 'Your straps are crooked . . . those stockings aren't straight . . . you shouldn't wear ties with pinafores . . . very smart . . . all right men, carry on.'

The next assignment started on 14 April when Andrew was one of 39 students entering the intensive course at Greenwich Royal Naval College for the Writer's Exam, involving defence policies and economics – considered essential for promotion in the Services. It was a hard, eight-week course and evenings were spent swotting up on lectures in his plainly furnished bed-sitting-room at the College.

On Monday 21 April Fergie undertook her first truly royal engagement on the occasion of the Queen's sixtieth birthday. The official photographs for the occasion had already been taken by Andrew at Sandringham and the family gathered at Windsor for a thanksgiving service at St George's Chapel; afterwards the Queen drove to London, where thousands of schoolchildren were to sing her a birthday song outside Buckingham Palace. To the delight of the crowd, on the balcony, along with the Queen Mother, the Prince and Princess of Wales, Princess Anne,

Prince Andrew and Prince Edward, stood Sarah Ferguson.

It was an extraordinary sight – six thousand children all waving daffodils and cheering. Fergie was visibly over-whelmed by the emotion of the cheering. It was with some difficulty that she gathered herself. However, by the time she joined the Queen for a walkabout among the children, Fergie had regained her composure, and was able to enjoy the magnificence of it all. That evening she became totally part of the family when, along with Diana, Sarah Armstrong-Jones and Helen Windsor, she went to the Royal Opera House for a gala evening of opera, ballet and music called 'Fanfare for a Queen' with Placido Domingo, Jessye Norman, Paul Eddington, Judi Dench and a host of other stars singing, dancing and talking.

Koo, like Banquo's ghost, continued to appear at the feast. Early in April the National Portrait Gallery, despite their earlier comments on her work, admitted that she had given them a portrait photograph of Prince Andrew with a full naval beard taken after his second tour of duty in the Falklands. The condition of the gift was that it should not be reproduced or sold.

Not all of Fergie's friends were totally happy about the way that the Palace had by now taken over her life. While some had chatty phone calls and letters from Fergie, some were mysteriously dropped, or didn't have their phone calls to the Palace returned. One said: 'It seems to be a Hanov-erian trait of taking over the poor girls who marry into the family. They leave them to be pilloried and persecuted and then move them in and keep them. Why should she get married from Clarence House? Why couldn't she get mar-ried in that pretty church in Dummer if she wants to and have a marquee in the garden, like Jane did? I never quite saw why Diana Spencer couldn't have got married from Spencer House in London in a Spencer coach.'

But Fergie was enjoying things far too much to worry about that. Major Ferguson was delighted not to have been asked to pay for anything ('It's a State occasion, isn't it?' he said) and Fergie, driving a new Jaguar Cabriolet she had been lent by the makers (the BMW, which she still had, was of course a German car), went shopping for new clothes: riding clothes for the royal family's traditional morning rides in Royal Ascot Week, dresses and swimwear for the week she and Florence Belmondo had arranged to spend at her father's villa in Antigua.

The arrangements had been made with some difficulty as Florence, who had married advertising man Larry-Neil Andrews and had been teaching aerobics, was in Seattle while Fergie was in London. But they met up and Fergie was glad to be away from the London pressures although, inevitably, many cameramen were sent over by the British press to cover the holiday. 'Reptiles,' was the succinct view of her father, who was far happier to think of the joy of having such a suitable new son-in-law: 'He's tough and he speaks straight and is a good, strong man in every sense of the word. He and Sarah will make a smashing team.'

11

The Big Day Approaches

That Antigua holiday made clearer than ever the figure-problems that now confronted Fergie. For if comparison to Diana was unfortunate, with Florence it was worse. While Florence Belmondo looked lithe and tanned in the skimpiest of bikinis, Fergie looked decidedly pale and large in her swimsuits – although she did take the sensible precaution of covering up with a large man's shirt when photographers were anywhere near.

She'd shown how genuinely nice she is when some Fleet Street reporters 'happened' to sit next to her and Florence one evening at The Admiral's Inn restaurant. She sent them a bunch of flowers from a vase on her table, and when they thanked her she apologised: 'I'm afraid I can't run to champagne. I'll have to speak to my boss in Geneva about a pay rise.' The journalists sent across a bottle of champagne, and she toasted them: 'Enjoy your holiday.' And as she left the restaurant, she asked the waiter to take the bottle back: 'We can't finish it. I'd like you to have some too.' As one of those pursuers says: 'What a delight she is. A lovely, lovely person. She didn't actually cooperate with us, but she did understand that we had a job to do.'

Fergie returned to a rather damp London and, after her first official engagement with Andrew at a charity gala in Weymouth, Dorset, she and Diana sat down to plan the wedding campaign. When Diana had first married she did not have any fashion sense – what she did have was an adviser with fashion sense who guided her along the first tricky paths. Fergie did have fashion sense, but it was a fashion sense tempered by her £12,000 a year salary. Suddenly she was like a child let loose in a big sweet shop and she did not know which way to turn. As many know to their cost, something that looks stunning on a tall, slender model girl in a glossy magazine will often look a mess on other people. Previously Fergie could only look and drool at the smart fashions, now she was a princess in the making and could have whatever she wanted.

She and Diana had already decided that the important thing was to create a wardrobe for Fergie that could not possibly be perceived as competition. Different advisers, different designers would, they both hoped, discourage too much comparison. So together they plotted and came up with a solution. While Diana had gone to Anna Harvey, one of the fashion editors at *Vogue*, Fergie went to Lucy Dickens, fashion and beauty editor of *Brides* magazine, also published by the Condé Nast company at the modern-looking Vogue House in Hanover Square, just around the corner from Fergie's office. The contrast between the two advisers was ideal: Anna is dark, in her thirties, of medium build, has two boys and a girl and lives in Wandsworth. Lucy is blonde, petite, in her twenties, has a parrot, no children and lives with her accountant husband in Dulwich.

Lucy Dickens had not come across Lindka Cierach, since *Brides* – correctly titled *Brides and Setting Up Home* – rarely features couture dressmakers and the dressmakers never contact the magazine as they don't have samples they can send around. As Fergie had already picked her dress-maker for the wedding gown, Lucy trawled the designers to find other items that might be suitable for Fergie. But there again, while *Vogue* found Diana's clothes for six months before the wedding and the first eight months afterwards, Lucy only did the initial searching and by the time of Royal Ascot Fergie was wearing things that were quite a surprise to her.

Fergie could look at samples at Vogue House and then visit the designers whose work she had liked. She went to the 30-year-old-Scot, Alistair Blair – whose assistant is

Viscount Linley's girlfriend, Susannah Constantine – for the outfit she wore for the official engagement announcement. Among the other young designers commissioned were Suzanne Schneider of Sujon, Catharine Walker of The Chelsea Design Company and, on a personal whim of Fergie's, the well-established Gina Fratini.

A major role was given to Paul Golding, a 27-year-old Oxford graduate and former architecture student, who was commissioned to create twenty-five outfits for her at his Georgian terraced house in Cheyne Walk, which doubles as home and workroom. Golding's views on fashion suited Fergie and he says: 'I do hate this craze for boyish, emaciated bodies. Women should look like women, not men. And my clothes are unashamedly classic. I design for the discerning woman, with a strong line in common sense, not clothes-aholics who are forever updating their wardrobes with the latest gimmick.'

Another source of ideas was the Argentinian Roberto Devorik, who owns thirteen shops in the West End and Knightsbridge headed by the Régine shops. Fergie had long admired the somewhat costly clothes in his Bond Street shop and considered that he would be a good adviser for a princess. And she was not the only one who enthused about the permanently tanned Devorik, for he was also asked to make dresses for the wedding by Susie Barrantes and Princess Michael.

For hats, she again hunted around, avoiding Diana's favourites and having several created by David Shilling, the flamboyant, good-humoured character who is probably best known for the outrageous Ascot hats he has made for his mother, Mrs Gertrude Shilling.

Fergie had not previously dressed to be noticed, but now that she realised it was expected of her, she quickly showed that she had a mind of her own. It might not always have been on the right lines, but at least it was her own.

Payment for this fashion extravaganza is a delicate matter. Invariably Fergie, like Diana on a shopping trip, will have things sent to Buckingham Palace. The shop will then send a bill, sometimes for the full amount, sometimes with a discount. Sometimes, even, suppliers will conveniently 'forget' to send a bill. The bargain shopping does not always work out as planned.

Fergie felt quite at home accompanying Andrew on his travels, and he enjoyed her company. Before he had found his public engagements an unenviable and rather lonely chore, but now all that was changed. The contrast to Charles and Diana, during their engagement, was remarkable. Charles and Diana had led quite separate existences, as though the bride were being kept cocooned in cotton wool before the ceremony. But Fergie, invariably sporting a bow in her hair, went everywhere and had the time of her life. Her natural enthusiasm shone through, and although at some later stage she may find it a strain keeping up a constant stream of good-natured banter, for the time being it was a doddle. Fergie positively radiated happiness and fun and Andrew seemed to mature by the day. Previously it had always been Prince Philip or Charles who had represented the public conscience of the royal family, but now Andrew began to take an open interest in social issues, writing his own speeches, lecturing city businessmen on the dangers of 'moral pollution' of British youth and shunning suggestions that he should postpone a planned trip to Northern Ireland. Prince Philip and the Queen could not conceal their new-found pride in their second son.

With Andrew spending most of his time on a course at Greenwich, Fergie seemed to be everywhere. While the Queen was away in Scotland, Fergie was the principal guest at the Queen's Cup polo finals at Smith's Lawn – won by Guy Wildenstein's Les Diables Bleus, with Charles playing at back in an extra-time match won 9–8 against shipping magnate Tony Embiricos' Tramonta team. Diana and Fergie had great fun, both arriving in polka dots – red spots with matching short socks for Diana and black spots for Fergie.

Together with Andrew Sarah presided at the opening of the Imperial War Museum's new £2 million extension at

Duxford, Cambridgeshire and in his speech Andrew admitted that he, like most other newly engaged young men, found it difficult to change from 'I' to 'We'. 'Oops, sorry, I've done it again,' he said, while Fergie, in mock horror, looked heavenwards.

Business was booming for Richard Burton SA, but Fergie found that her new enthusiasm for everything gave her great reserves of energy and she could cope easily with her regular work load most mornings at Buckingham Palace or sometimes at Sotheby's offices – which also acted as a mail drop-off point – before going off on shopping expeditions or on her regular duties. She managed to cover the annual Grosvenor House Antiques Fair early one morning in the third week of June, greeting old friends and making new contacts, before heading off to meet her mother who had just arrived in London with Hector from Brant's Greenwich farm, via New York.

The next day, at the start of Royal Ascot week, the world was able to see just how much difference one year had made. From being someone who had merely gone along for the ride, Fergie was now the star of the show, the girl that everyone wanted to see.

This time it was Prince Andrew who drove her down to Windsor Castle, where she was warmly welcomed by the Queen and the whole array of staff. She was given a large guest suite of rooms near to the prince's own bedroom – there could still be no question of them sharing a room. She had brought her new riding outfits, specially made for her at Gidden's, the Queen's saddlers, for the early morning rides with the Queen. 'I'll need to look good,' she said, 'so I must have some new things.' But it was sad that she had no chance to show off the outfits, which included a particularly smart new pair of white riding jodphurs with the old-fashioned wide seat, since there was an outbreak of ringworm at the Windsor Castle stables.

The Tuesday, first day of the Ascot meeting, was sunny and hot, a blessed relief after the rain-sodden spring. For the coach ride down the course from the castle Andrew travelled with Charles, the Queen and Prince Philip to the racetrack; intriguingly both Philip and Andrew wore black morning coats and black top hats while Charles wore a more fashionable – and somewhat cooler – grey top hat and morning suit. Andrew wore a dun-coloured double breasted waistcoat as well, but by the Thursday he had swopped his black top hat for a grey one. Mrs Gertrude Shilling, a Royal Ascot regular with her outrageous confections, wore a two and a half-foot hat with a piano keyboard marked on it and a black on white silk dress that was embroidered with the opening bars of the Wedding March from Wagner's Lohengrin, 'In honour of Prince Andrew and Sarah Ferguson,' she explained. When Diana spotted the hat she could not help bursting into giggles, all the more so because she knew something that others did not. Fergie, who rode in a coach with Princess Anne, wore a turquoise and white gingham-checked sailor-suit outfit by Paul Golding with an elegant white hat with a halo-like brim that met with universal admiration and approval. Diana was one of the very few who knew that Fergie's hat was designed by David Shilling, in complete contrast to the monstrous joke worn by his mother.

Susie and Hector Barrantes were also at Ascot and were guests of the Queen in the Royal Box. The most extraordinary precautions were taken to ensure that the Barrantes couple – Susie with her long blonde hair, far longer than her daughter's, flowing under her hat in the sun – could both enter the Royal Enclosure and arrive at the Royal Box with the minimum of attention from the phalanx of photographers who stood on the first floor balcony outside the Enclosure – cameras are not allowed inside.

Andrew and Fergie followed Prince Charles and Diana to the Guards Polo Club after the racing, to find that Major Ferguson had accidentally been struck above his left eye by a polo mallet and had a large plaster and pad over it, although 'The Major', as he is called even by his wife, made light of his injury and said: 'I've had far worse things happen in thirty-two years of playing polo.' Major

Ferguson (otherwise Ron or Ronald, never Ronnie, and many consider it bad form for a retired officer to continue using his rank) is actually Deputy-Chairman of the Guards Polo Club, but is invariably known as 'Polo-Stick-In-Waiting' because of his role organising the royal family's preferred sport.

The Wednesday of Ascot week was a bad one for Fergie's fashion confidence. Her outfit – navy and lime green with wide, white slashes across it – had overtones of a Japanese warrior. Together with the pillbox hat perched on her hair which she wore up, it was universally criticised. It looked frumpy, was the consensus, although Andrew did declare that he liked it, whatever others might say. Paul Golding defended the dress: 'It is a strong dress and I expected strong reaction.' On Day Three, Ladies' Day, Fergie recovered her poise with a floral silk-satin dress with a square neck, a V-point belt at the waist and gathered, leg o' mutton shoulders worn with a plain aquamarine silk/satin jacket and a wide-brimmed sombrero hat. On the Friday, when Fergie wore a deep purple silk suit, cut low at the front, and a lilac-and-white hat with a transparent brim, there was some competition for attention when Koo Stark arrived. Had she applied to the Lord Chamberlain's office for Royal Enclosure vouchers in the normal way she would have been issued with a badge in her married name, but as it was she had made the arrangements through Andrew and was given a badge that announced Miss Kathleen Stark. There was no denying that she looked particularly pretty and demure in a plain navy outfit with striped lapels and her hair plaited. She wore a simple matching hat with a striped hatband, little makeup and a ruby stud mounted on silver in the left side of her nose; her whole appearance only emphasised the difference between herself and Fergie. She was cool, pretty, a little exotic; Fergie was flowery, enthusiastic, very traditional.

At this time a flood of publications appeared about the couple, from *The Royal Wedding Official Souvenir*, published 'by Gracious Permission of Her Majesty The

Queen', sold for £2.25 in aid of King George's Jubilee Trust for the benefit of children affected by fatal or crippling diseases, to a brochure called *Sarah Ferguson's Hampshire Home, Dummer Village*, with a commentary written by Anne Pitcher and including old pictures of village life and photographs from the Ferguson family album, that was sold by the Royal College of Obstetricians for £3.00 to benefit the Birthright charity – Susan Ferguson had recently become its secretary for the Basingstoke area.

The official brochure included photographs taken by fashion photographer Terence Donovan, a big bruiser of a man who made his name in the David Bailey days of Cockney rough trade photographers. Donovan is a powerfully-built judo black belt; his pictures of the prince, wearing a 1930s style gangster's double-breasted suit with wide chalk stripes – particularly those poses in which Andrew has his hand in his jacket pocket – rather emphasise Andrew's own beefy look, but they certainly make a change from the run-of-the-mill royal portraits. Andrew wore a blue tie to match their eyes and Fergie's floral frock by Suzanne Schneider and the decor of the ornate White Drawing Room at Buckingham Palace. Beneath his gruff exterior Donovan is a gentle man and was surprised to be asked to do the session – modestly, and jokingly, he put the commission down to the fact that he was one of the few photographer's to praise Andrew's published book of photographs publicly. He said that he found some aspects of the session unusual: 'Of course it was exacting work – not only is one half of the team a photographer, but he also has that extraordinary eyesight that pilots have which makes you look round a bit more yourself.' He waived all payment to increase the benefit to the charity. For the formal poses, Andrew wore his ceremonial naval dress uniform with the aiguillettes on his right shoulder that denote his position as personal aide-de-camp to the Queen, the insignia of the Companion of the Victorian Order around his neck, and on his left Shoulder the Jubilee Medal and the South Atlantic Medal, with the rosette on the ribbon to show that he was actually in the exclusion zone during the Falklands war.

The style of the photographs cannot be faulted, but unwisely Fergie wore the Alistair Blair evening gown which had been so admired by the Queen when Fergie had attended her 60th birthday gala at Covent Garden, with her hair up in a chignon. The royal blue satin dress has a rather unfortunate white top that would, as one fashion expert said, 'look good on Audrey Hepburn.' On Fergie it made her look large and matronly. But as if to make up for that, there was a particularly warm and relaxed portrait of them both taken by Gene Nocon, from the same session that produced the portrait the Post Office used for their commemorative stamps, as well as a delightful picture of Fergie taken by Andrew himself.

By this time the London Diamond Centre were selling a £5,000 replica of Fergie's ring. There were cups, mugs and suchlike in abundance and, for £25.50, a handsome heraldic canvas embroidery outfit depicting Fergie's coat of arms. Invitations to the wedding were the most desirable thing around town: Nancy Reagan, whom Andrew had become friendly with on his trips to America and her trips here, said that she would have no hesitation in bucking the trend of Americans, concerned about terrorism, not to come to Britain. And there were ways and means of getting an invitation. American cosmetics millionairess Estée Lauder, who had been an enthusiastic and lavish supporter of polo, was invited by Major Ferguson. Some of the British folk wanting to attend the wedding ensured a place by having sent congratulatory bouquets as soon as the engagement was announced. Most of these flower senders were rewarded with an invitation. Friends of Susie Ferguson from the United States were invited and so were Andrew's model girlfriends.

What could they give a couple who have everything? Guided by the Palace, who explained that those who wanted to give lavish presents, might be offended if the couple only listed cheap items, they followed the example of Charles and Diana as well as that of many of their friends and started a wedding list at the General Trading Company in Sloane Street. Suggested gifts ranged from the cheap – a Dartington vase at £3.95 – ; the fun mugs with little teddy bears on them; to the expensive – a Georgian table at £3,150 with reproduction chairs at £2,346. At Asprey's in Bond Street there were more extravagant items, such as a sterling silver canteen for almost £14,000 or a range of leather luggage at £1,000. Fergie requested that furniture – she suggested a total of eight sofas – should be from the interior designers Charles Hammond in Sloane Street and covered in white calico, so that she could have them upholstered later. Thomas Goode & Co of South Audley Street, Mayfair, would provide glass and china.

For Fergie the whole period was one of tremendous enjoyment and excitement. She flew to the Isle of Wight for an air race, went to Queen's Tennis Tournament, and to Wimbledon, and on 26 June she accompanied Andrew to Belfast to open a £72 million showpiece block at Belfast City Hospital. From London they flew to RAF Aldergrove, before flying by helicopter to Newforge Playing Fields, South Belfast. Despite the security and information clampdown they were greeted by some 2,000 children. They had a full schedule, meeting Ulster Loyalist MP Ian Paisley's daughter Rhonda, who is Belfast's Lady Mayor, before travelling eighteen miles to the Antrim sports centre for the Royal Ulster Constabulary's sports day. In the evening they visited Killyleagh Yacht Club before spending the night with Ulster Secretary Tom King at Hillsborough Castle. They next travelled to the small village of Upperlands in County Londonderry where Fergie toured the 250-year-old linen factory of William Clark & Sons, which has stood by the winding River Claudy through eight generations of the same family. The company had had a particular reason for inviting her to visit and were quite astounded when their request for a visit from her was fulfilled so speedily. As Wallace Clark, marketing director of the firm, explained, her forebear Dr James Ferguson, a Belfast linen manufacturer, had married in 1750 as his second wife,

Sarah Clark, who was the daughter of the firm's founder. Fergie was genuinely surprised to hear of her connection with the family and it was only on her return to England that her father explained the relevance of the Irish Fergusons and her new coat of arms.

But next day when they visited a police convalescence home in Harrogate both Andrew and Fergie, wearing a pretty, spotted outfit, were suffering from hay fever and with the general pollen count in the area around a high of 200 they were somewhat overcome by the mass of flowers offered to them. 'Oh no, not more flowers,' said Andrew, while Fergie consoled him: 'We'll get used to it.'

Fergie confessed to one inmate that Andrew had told her three times to shut up as she was getting over-excited. But there was so much to do. And Fergie's appetite for life was continually fuelled. With Andrew at the controls of a red Wessex helicopter of the Queen's Flight she flew in – and out – of Castle Ashby House in Northamptonshire to watch a five-country (Britain, America, West Germany, Poland and Russia) helicopter championship. Then they flew to North Wales for a charity shooting event. Using a 12-bore gun and equipped with ear protection Andrew hit six out of seven clays while Fergie failed four times to hit a stationary plastic rabbit. But she had great fun.

The only unhappiness in their lives at this time was when Fergie heard that Eduardo Moore, who used to play alongside Hector Barrantes for Sam Vestey, had shot himself at his farm near Buenos Aires. Like Barrantes he had only stopped playing in Britain during the Falklands war. From his property-dealing and breeding of top class polo ponies, the dashingly good-looking Moore had made a deal of money; unhappily he had also lost a lot in unwise investments and it was the money worries that finally led him to take his own life.

Meanwhile the wedding preparations had been pressing ahead. Andrew and Fergie had quietly visited Westminster Abbey when it was closed for the Order of the Bath ceremony, so that they could get an idea of the place with the big blue carpet rolled out. Andrew and Fergie had meetings with the Archbishop of Canterbury, Dr Robert Runcie, to discuss the form of the service. Fergie and Andrew, unable to believe that anyone could have ever thought the engagement was too short, could hardly wait for their wedding day.

12

The Wedding

Pageantry, pomp and ceremony. Without a doubt it is what the British do best in the whole world. And every last drop of magic, emotion, happiness, laughter and tears, was wrung from millions on that Wednesday 23 July. It was not a Public Holiday, but you would never have guessed. Many were given the day off work, and those who were not were glued to television sets in shops and offices and little work was done while the wedding was on.

There had been plenty of light-hearted moments leading up to the event. A few days earlier, Fergie and Diana, dressed as policewomen, had decided, along with Pamela Stephenson, to raid Andrew's stag night dinner, but had been foiled in the attempt by press men waiting outside the venue at the Camden Hill Square home of Richard Lascelles. Instead they decided to call into Annabel's in Berkeley Square for a nightcap, where, amazingly, they went undetected. Pamela Stephenson had arranged the gag, hiring the costumes from theatrical costumiers Berman and Nathan's, whose Monty Berman enthusiastically said that he would never have let the uniforms go except for filming. Diana reported that her outfit was far too small. 'The wig made me hot and uncomfortable. I couldn't wait to take it off. And my black shoes were two sizes too small.' She explained the prank with, 'you have to have a laugh sometimes.'

The stag night itself was a mixture of fun and seriousness, but the guest list was further indication of the problem Andrew had in making his own friends. The guest list included naval officers, a few school friends, and Billy Connolly, Elton John and David Frost – unofficial courtiers as much as friends. Elton John sang, Billy Connolly had a few stories up his sleeve and four young ladies were hired to provide 'bachelor entertainment' of quite a modest sort.

Then on the Thursday before the wedding, Madame Tussaud's unveiled their waxworks version of Fergie, modelled by Karen Newman, at their Baker Street showrooms – one irreverent photographer whipped out a tape measure which he ran around the hips and announced that they measured 44 inches, less perhaps two inches for clothes, estimating 42 inches. The sculptress would not be drawn.

On the Monday Prince Edward turned up for the Abbey rehearsals wearing a sling on his left arm. ('He was bitten by a kiwi,' a poker faced Squadron Leader Adam Wise, Prince Andrew's equerry, explained) and on his right arm when he departed.

The royal family don't have regular wedding receptions; they usually give a dance for friends a few days beforehand and a wedding breakfast for the close family (about 200) at Buckingham Palace. This time it was Ronald Ferguson himself who hosted a dinner and dance in a large marquee at Smith's Lawn, the Guards Polo Club headquarters, for the royal family and friends – even Susie and Hector Barrantes were there.

The dinner and dance, the wedding dress itself and the bridesmaids and page boys outfits were Ronald Ferguson's contributions to the wedding – and pretty hefty ones, too. The Ferguson family is comfortable, but not hugely rich and Ronald Ferguson earns less than £20,000 a year for his Guards Club duties. Dummer Down House, his '£2 million' home, is a rather plain, but comfortable Hampshire house. While it is true that if Fergie's father did sell his house and 800 acre farm he might get £2 million for it – farm land does still fetch that kind of money, although it gives a paltry return on capital – there would be no home, no place for the ponies and nowhere for Fergie, Andrew and, one day, their children to go. One of Fergie's attractions to Andrew is that she is, on his terms, part of a normal family. No actual cost of the splendour of the wedding itself could be calculated – even many millions could not buy the arrangements, the troops, the street closure, the police and the security involved.

On the eve of the wedding there had been the almost traditional royal interview – although it was Charles and Diana who first suffered this indignity. To play fair, Andrew Gardner of Thames for ITV and Sue Lawley for BBC shared the interview. Andrew and Fergie romped through it all, but if they suffered, they suffered gallantly. Fergie was shown discussing and inspecting her wardrobe – row upon row of new dresses and a huge cupboard full of £100 per time Manolo Blahnik shoes (she must have spent more on clothes in the last six months than she has in the previous 25 years.) But Fergie, padding around the corridors of Buckingham Palace in her stockinged feet was completely at ease.

She explained why there was the traditional 'obey' in the service. 'Andrew's the boss,' she said, although observers had already noted that brides who readily agree to say 'obey' in the service are often fairly self-willed types who have every intention of going their own way afterwards – it was the idea of Prince Charles under the guidance of the Archbishop of Canterbury who suggested that Diana should omit it. 'I was thinking of obeying in the moral terms as opposed to the physical terms,' Fergie said. 'Andrew will make the decision because he is the man of the marriage. Therefore in that sense I will obey him at one stage or another.' And she added, 'I am not the person to obey meekly.'

She was ebullient, enthusiastic and obviously excited and happy for herself and for Andrew. They walked hand in hand, were seen on engagements and were interviewed sitting on the yellow sofa of Andrew's sitting room. 'I'm so excited. Fantastic! The more the merrier – more carriages, more pomp. Wonderful, I love it. It's our wedding. We have made the final decision. Every decision is made by us. The music, the service and the ceremony.' She defended the Fergie figure, saying, 'I do not diet, I do not have a problem. A woman should have a trim waist, a good "up top" and enough down the bottom – a good womanly figure. I dress for Andrew and only for Andrew. I am not a great clothes horse.' Andrew backed her up, 'I said to Sarah right from the word go – when we were first engaged – buy your clothes for yourself, not for anybody else.' They confessed to having no home after their honeymoon and Andrew explained, 'finding a house is a long-term plan rather than a short-term desire.'

There were questions as to whether they wanted to live in the 'Gloucestershire triangle' where Princess Anne, Prince Charles and Prince Michael all have homes. 'No,' said Fergie quickly, exchanging a glance with Andrew. 'But a house south of the M4 would be nice.' Andrew laughed. 'The difficulty is that being in the Navy one is generally based in the South. But I too would rather not be in Gloucestershire – I think it is slightly overcrowded!'

About her future as a princess, Fergie was unruffled, 'You do get better service in shops' – and according to Andrew her new life would not be a problem. 'Having seen her diary I couldn't have kept up with the pace. She was fantastic.'

Wednesday 23 July dawned in that slightly overcast way that is the precursor of a very hot day, a very wet day or . . . just sometimes, one of those neither one thing nor the other thing days. And that's the way it was. Bursts of sunshine occasionally lit the scene, sometimes small showers fell. Warm enough for the onlookers, cool enough for the soldiers in their full ceremonial uniforms.

The troopers had been polishing their breastplates and preparing their horses from 4 am; from 6 am everyone concerned was wide awake and active, policemen were lining the route, SAS squads, many undercover, patrolled the rooftops in search of terrorists wanting to spoil the day. So concerned were Scotland Yard that there might be

some outrage that they took extraordinary precautions –
troopers were wired up to a central contact point, armed
detectives pulled on their uniforms as coachmen to ride on
the back of each carriage, and the five miles of sewers under
Westminster were checked.

Fergie had had an early night at Clarence House, slept
well and woke early. Lindka Cierach had already delivered
the dress, hairdresser Denise McAdam arrived before
9 am, as did her manicurist the twenty-year-old Beverley
Nathan, also from Michaeljohn. Thirty-five-year-old
make-up artist Teresa Fairminder was there from her
Chiswick home – the wedding make-up would be light,
similar to the way that Fergie normally wears it. Her
mother, Susie Barrantes – the first Mrs Ferguson is always
Susie, the second is called Susan – was another early
arrival, very elegantly dressed in gold with her long hair
piled high under a matching wide-brimmed gold hat.

Poet Laureate Ted Hughes had penned a poem, in his
particular mixture of modern language and nature ter-
minology, called *The Honey Bee and The Thistle*, named
after Fergie's crest and chronicling the romance. And there
was an announcement from Buckingham Palace, pinned to
the railings at 10 am. The Queen was pleased to confer on
her second son the titles of Duke of York, Earl of Inverness
and Baron Killyleagh – one English title, one Scottish and
one Irish, named after the Co. Down town home of
Fergie's forebears. Now when Fergie was actually married
she would become Duchess of York, and she couldn't but
remember that twice this century the Duchess of York had
later become Queen. Andrew and Fergie's children would
be Prince or Princess of York. Their eldest grandson would
take the title Earl of Inverness.

Even as the announcement was posted, and the 1,800
guests – some 720 on Andrew and Fergie's own list – for the
service had started to arrive at the Abbey, the good natured
crowds, some of whom had been waiting on the streets for
several days to ensure the most advantageous positions,
began to sing *The Grand Old Duke of York*, cheering

each new arrival at the church amidst the carefree, carnival atmosphere that was in the air.

The prince's showbusiness favourites like Billy Connolly, Pamela Stephenson, Elton John, Michael Caine, David Frost and Anthony Andrews made their way to their places. The politicians and their spouses, Margaret and Denis Thatcher, David and Debbie Owen, David Steel, William Whitelaw, Lord Hailsham, and Neil and Glynis Kinnock – Labour party leader Kinnock getting no marks for diplomacy by wearing a blue lounge suit rather than a morning suit.

There were work colleagues from the Navy and Fergie's friends from her past and present life. Also present were old flames, such as Paddy McNally, with his children, brother and even parents, Kim Smith-Bingham and his wife, Fiona. Even Andrew's Canadian teenage crush Sandi Jones and her brother Peter were there, along with Katie Rabett and other pretty girls from the past. Only Koo Stark was absent: she had not been invited, but diplomatically told friends she was going to America for a short while.

By horse-drawn carriage the Queen and her family started to leave the Palace – all the ladies seemingly dressed in blue (except for Princess Anne, in yellow), as though off to be photographed by Norman Parkinson for a family group. The Queen, looking particularly smart in an elegant blue dress, carried a matching clutch handbag rather than the more traditional handled type. Then from Buckingham Palace, Prince Andrew, now the Duke of York, gloveless, in his naval uniform, wearing the Queen's Jubilee Medal, the Falklands Medal and the star around the neck of a Commander of the Royal Victorian Order. By his side in the 1902 State Landau was his brother and Supporter (as the Royal Family call their Best Man), Prince Edward, in his Royal Marine Lieutenant's uniform and wearing the Jubilee Medal.

At a minute or so before 11.15 Fergie adjusted the dress, checked the small blue bow sewn on to her silk underwear and came down the grand stairs at Clarence House to meet her father, who was dressed in his grandfather's braided morning suit that he had worn at both his own marriages, with a small red rose bud buttonhole picked that morning from his garden in Dummer ('I asked Sarah if she wanted me to get a new one and she said "Not on your life – I want you to wear that."')

Ferguson could not help but look at the floating dream of embroidered ivory duchesse satin in amazement and not for the last time that day, they both had to wipe away a tear as it came to their eye. Later that day Ferguson had found some words again: 'She took my breath away. She looked quite, quite wonderful.' Father and daughter having climbed aboard aided by Lindka, coachman John Nelson took the 1881 Glass Coach, out of the black gates of Clarence House at a brisk trot and the world got a first glimpse of the dress, with its scalloped veil held under a floral headband, with her glorious Titian hair, tightly crimped but worn loose, flowing underneath.

Royal brides travelling in the Glass Coach are customarily escorted by a mounted police guard; at Ronald Ferguson's own request on this occasion there was an escort of six Life Guards, the regiment of Ferguson, his father and grandfather, and the regiment in which in 1961 and 1967 he had been Squadron Leader and Captain of the Queen's Escort for Trooping the Colour.

Fergie and her father chatted, in awe and amazement at the crowds cheering their progress and Fergie waved energetically to all and sundry. Before they knew it, they had travelled the short journey down the Mall, through Admiralty Arch, along Whitehall and through Parliament Square to Westminster Abbey, festooned in gold, pink and peach roses and gardenias wafting a sweet scent through the air.

At 11.20 – these royal functions are run very precisely and Fergie's suggestion that she should be five minutes late at the church was quickly dismissed by palace officials – the Glass Coach arrived at the Abbey. For the first time the full splendour of the satin dress, was in view with its 17½ feet of

train embroidered with a large 'A' and entertwined 'S's'
and embroidered anchors. (Lindka Cierach had actually
made two identical dresses – the other one for Madame
Tussaud's new Fergie waxwork). 'There will never be
another dress like it,' Fergie had said – and there won't be.
Estimates of the time taken to sew incredible seed pearl
embroidery, so much a part of the Cierach work, were
many, many hours and as Lindka said, 'It will be the
greatest dress I ever make.'

Lindka Cierach, in neat black and white, had been
whisked by car from Clarence House, arriving before
Fergie at the Abbey. She carefully arranged the skirt and
ensured the train was in order – unfortunately failing to
notice that Fergie's diamond necklace was not quite
straight. The small attendants comprised of Prince William, four, and Jane Makim's five-year-old son Seamus
wearing little Victorian-style sailor suits, Fergie's seven-
year-old half-brother Andrew Ferguson and Princess
Anne's son Peter Phillips, eight, in Midshipmen's full dress
uniform of 1782. They were each hand in hand with one of
the little girls, William with Princess Anne's daughter Zara
Phillips, four; Seamus with Fergie's half-sister Alice, five;
Andrew with Robert Fellowes' daughter Laura, six; and
Peter with the senior bridesmaid, seven-year-old Lady
Rosanagh Innes-Ker, invariably known as Rosie and nicknamed 'Rosebud' by her father, the Earl of Roxburghe.
The boys' uniforms, like Andrew's and Edward's, were
made by Gieves and Hawkes in Savile Row. The girls wore
ivory frocks to complement the bridal gown, with flowers in
their hair and carried floral hoops, while the two younger
boys (especially William) played with the cords of their
sailor hats.

The bouquet, the floral headdress and the flowers for the
attendants had been masterminded by the young St James's
florist Jane Packer and made by royal florists Longman's,
and had been chosen from three separate versions sent
earlier to the palace. An exact copy of the bridal bouquet
was delivered direct to Buckingham Palace at 11 am

to be fresh and uncrumpled for the formal photographic session.

Fergie, a mite nervous, for the first time turned to her father, smiled, and said 'do you know the way?' He joked back, 'I'm following the blue,' as the massive fanfare from the trumpeters of the Royal Marines was followed by the powerful organ music of Edward Elgar's *Imperial March* Fergie, holding tightly on to her father's arm, was still not the most graceful of walkers, but the dress, the train and the circumstances made her float up towards the High Altar as if in a dream.

As Andrew came out of the side chapel with Edward he glanced backwards briefly to check that Fergie was there and gave a quick smile of pleasure and joy.

Westminster Abbey is the most glorious and awe inspiring of churches on an ordinary day. En fête it is doubly magnificent. So it was for Andrew and Fergie. The music was rousing – *Praise to the Lord, the Almighty, the King of creation* – was the first hymn, before the Dean of the Abbey intoned the familiar words:

'Dearly beloved, we are gathered here in the sight of God and in the face of his congregation, to join together this man and this woman in Holy Matrimony.'

One breakthrough, and one on which the couple, eager to share their happiness agreed, was the installation of a remote-controlled camera high above the altar so that, for the first time at a royal wedding, the faces of the couple could be seen as they took their vows.

The Queen had long since taken out her reading glasses so that she could join in the singing and it was with a look of particular pleasure that she listened intently as Prince Charles read the lesson, from the third chapter of St Paul's Epistle to the Ephesians:

'For this cause I bow my knees unto the Father of Our Lord Jesus Christ, Of whom the whole family of heaven and earth is named, That he would grant you, according to the riches of his glory, to be strengthened with might by his Spirit in the inner man.'

There followed another rousing hymn, chosen by Fergie because of the naval connotations: 'Lead us, heavenly Father, lead us, o'er the world's tempestuous sea; guard us, guide us, keep us, feed us, for we have no help but thee; yet possessing every blessing, if our God our Father be.'

To make a truly ecumenical service there were prayers said by the Roman Catholic Archbishop of Westminster, Cardinal Basil Hume, from the Moderator of the General Assembly of the Church of Scotland, Professor Robert Craig, the Moderator of the Free Church Federal Council, Dr Donald English, the Chaplain of the Fleet, Archdeacon Noel Jones, and the Archbishop of York, Dr John Habgood.

William Walton's anthem, *Set me a seal upon thine heart*, was sung quite beautifully by the choir (the adult members of which made over £2,000 each for their work that day) before the hymn, *Come down, O Love divine, seek thou this soul of mine*.

As the couple squeezed into the chapel where the register was to be signed, soprano Felicity Lott, hatless, sang Mozart's *Laudate Dominum* and the American soprano Arleen Auger, also hatless, sang Mozart's *Exultate Dominum*.

The register was signed by all the close members of the royal family, bridesmaids and the pages, and the bride, now more relaxed, and her proud groom eased out of the side chapel, her necklace now straight and Andrew helping her adjust her train. In the nave Andrew gave a small formal bow to the Queen, as Fergie, with a smile as big as all outdoors, sank into a deep curtsey. The Queen, who as head of the Church of England does not allow herself to smile in church, could not help but give a smile of acknowledgment and pleasure.

The procession back to the Palace was a joyful and even more relaxed one. Fergie waved furiously, Andrew waved enthusiastically.

Ronald Ferguson followed in a carriage with the Queen: he was a little stiff and aware of keeping back so that the

Queen could be seen. Behind them came Prince Philip and Susie Barrantes, chatting animatedly.

Back at the Palace came one of the most touching sights of the day. As the bride and groom alighted, young Andrew Ferguson went to kiss Prince Andrew and his sister. Now all the pages and bridesmaids wanted kisses from everyone, and they all deserved them, for they had, barring a bit of frolicking from William, behaved impeccably. They had to be calmed down once again as there was much organisation for the set group photographs to be taken by Scots-born Albert Watson, to many a surprise choice, although in America he does share the same agent as the Earl of Snowdon. Watson had been among a number of photographers recommended by Gene Nocon and he is well known and much respected for his fashion photography and portraiture in New York where he now lives and works. Nocon would assist him, as well as taking his own informal shots throughout the day for Andrew's personal album.

The photographs had to be taken before the balcony appearance of the whole family. The crowd, surging down the Mall, was patient and gave a great roar of enthusiasm when the couple finally appeared. 'What was that?' said both Andrew and Fergie, although Andrew had heard perfectly well what they wanted. The chant was insistent – 'we want the kiss, kiss, kiss . . .' Andrew had been the one to encourage Charles to kiss his bride, so it was hardly surprising that the same was expected of him and he knew it.

So kiss they did. A real smacker, that kept everyone happy.

In time the family went in, although Andrew and Fergie first returned for a balcony appearance by themselves, to join the family and very close friends – 140, in all.

The wedding breakfast was a relaxed and informal affair, with lobster, lamb, and strawberries and cream arranged in the shape of the St George's Cross on a base of strawberry fool, along with Piesporter Goldtropfchen Auslese 1976.

Château Langoa-Barton 1976, Bollinger champagne and Graham's Port 1966. There were speeches, toasts and much laughter before Andrew drew his sword and together with his duchess, cut one of the tiers of the five tier wedding cake. The cake had weighed 240 pounds, and was 12 inches taller than the one baked for Prince Charles and made by three chefs at HMS Raleigh, the Navy supply school at Torpoint in Cornwall, had made the 250 mile journey to London three days earlier, packed in wooden packing cases. There had been a spare, identical cake on standby in case of any disaster, but that could now go to navy lads.

Other wedding breakfasts were celebrated across London. As one guest put it, 'that's the problem with royal weddings, there's nowhere to go afterwards.' They talked of the guests, particularly of Nancy Reagan, wearing a blue outfit almost exactly like the one the Queen had worn to Charles's wedding. They talked of the former lovers, the showbusiness folk. They talked of the dress, universally admired and a triumph of dressmaking. A regular coutourier might have designed the dress and tried to squeeze Fergie in; Lindka had built it around her. They talked of her progress, the happy faces and huge eyes she had made at her friends as she walked down the nave, the wink she had given Princess Diana – might not her apparent confidence and huge enjoyment of it all become a little wearing? But it was decided generally that Diana had been a shy little girl who had grown maybe too strong – although in the church she did look pensive and was rather suffering from the bad posture slouch that is common to many tall girls. Fergie on the other hand might seem to be totally confident, but those who knew her best said that underneath it all she was still insecure and that it was just so lovely to see her enjoying it all.

Fergie changed into a blue Suzanne Schneider dress to leave the Palace, Andrew wore a quiet suit and a contented, mission accomplished, look on his face. There wasn't much quietness outside. The Landau on the forecourt had been decorated with union jacks, a heart-shaped silver balloon, 'L' plates, a model satellite dish and a notice saying 'Phone Home' – relevant to Ronald Ferguson, who had complained that now his daughter was married she would not phone home. Diana was insistent that he should not have too easy a ride, and had persuaded an equerry to lash into the carriage a special present acquired by Prince Edward – a three foot teddy bear, 'so that you won't be lonely when Andrew's away at sea.'

Although some of the onlookers received occasional soakings from showers, each time that Andrew and Fergie ventured outside the weather was miraculously fine.

As the royal family, with the Queen smiling broadly (and rescuing Prince William from running under the carriage wheels), waved them off, one important person, Fergie's mother, kept in the background, maintaining the aloof and dignified silence she had always held. Rather like Diana's mother Frances Shand-Kydd (who, incidentally, at the age of 17 had turned down a proposal of marriage from Ronald Ferguson), Susie could see that she could be of most use to the bride by keeping her thoughts to herself and remaining with Hector, the man she loved, in the background of her daughter's big day.

Seen off by the royal family and friends and showered with 24,000 rose petals, the new Duke and Duchess set off just after 4 o'clock in the open Landau along Buckingham Palace Road and up Pimlico Road to the Royal Hospital in Chelsea where a red helicopter of the Queen's Flight awaited. From there they flew to Heathrow, where a Queen's Flight BA 146 aircraft with 'Just Married' written on the rear air brakes, was waiting to whisk them to the Azores, the sun-kissed group of islands 7,000 miles off the coast of Portugal, where the Royal Yacht Britannia awaited them as a haven from prying eyes and a fitting vessel to take Prince and Princess Andrew, Duke and Duchess of York, off into the new adventures of married life.

Fergie had told her inquisitors that her big ambition was to learn to fly – both fixed wing and rotary planes (that's what the professionals call helicopters). She had done quite a lot of flying that day: she had woken as a commoner and went to bed as a royal duchess.

Fergie had told a waiting official in the Azores how she felt: 'I have never, in all my life, been so happy.'

Epilogue

For the foreseeable future Andrew intends to carry on with his naval career. He's good at his job and there is no reason why he should not rise fast. However, the modern, highly specialised Navy is very different from the old one where an officer could amble along until retirement. Nowadays he has to rise in the system, or else he has to leave.

There could be difficult moments in the future if Andrew were to be one of two candidates up before a promotion board. Even if they prefer him on merit, there will be those who will think he was chosen because he is the Queen's son and because the selection board themselves were seeking preferment. Equally, if they reject him they risk being accused of dealing with him unfairly. But for the moment Andrew is determined to continue being his own man in a career in which, despite requiring new technical qualifications all the time, he is thriving. And he is totally supported in this by his wife. As her father says: 'He's good at his job. A professional. And he'll stick to it and Sarah won't mind at all. There's no point in being married to a frustrated husband.'

As for Fergie, she will not be short of things to do while he is at sea. She has already been inundated by charities, worthy organisations, at least one regiment and many others with requests for her to join them as patron. She enjoys her work with Richard Burton SA and wants to be able to continue with that in peace. Business has already improved severalfold since her engagement and she, being a practical sort, does not see why it couldn't expand some more. The *Palace of Westminster* book has to be completed – publication is planned for October – and Richard Burton is happy to work around her schedule. He continues to fly to London for regular meetings and sees no reason why that should stop, although he will undoubtedly have to acquire larger offices, if only to accommodate the private policeman now in Fergie's retinue.

Andrew's Civil List income – which he has been drawing since 1983, also has his officer's salary of £15,000 and his private income – now goes up from £20,000 to £50,000, which he is expected to take advantage of. Fergie will want and need an extensive wardrobe as she will be expected to present herself well, although she has always been quite careful with money before and she will undoubtedly remain so now.

And what do the stars hold for Andrew and Fergie? To get a full and accurate picture of the astrological make-up of the relationship, it was necessary for complete charts to be prepared, from which experts could draw the fullest conclusions. To ensure the validity of the readings, the experts did not initially know the names of the people whose charts they were interpreting, and futures they were casting, although they did know that they were investigating a union of two people on a given day. The results are fascinating.

Fergie, a Libran, was born on 15 October 1959 at 9.03 a.m. at 27 Welbeck Street, London, with the Sun in Libra and the Moon in Aries.

Andrew, a Piscean, was born four months later at 3.30 p.m. on 19 February 1960 at Buckingham Palace, with the Sun in Aquarius and the Moon in Scorpio.

Looking first to the East and the Chinese lunar calendar, Andrew was born in the Year of the Rat, with the Fixed Element of Metal, and Fergie was born in the year of the Boar, with the Fixed Element of Earth.

The Chinese wisdom, distilled from the time of the calendar's introduction by the Emperor Huang in 2637 BC, is that Andrew, as a Rat, is easy to get on with, hard-working and thrifty. He cherishes his family and friends and his emotional commitments are lasting ones. On the minus side, the Rat can be tricky, will criticise unnecessarily and be careful with his wealth, although that is unlikely to be the case with Andrew. The Rat enjoys pageantry and pomp and will do his best to advance himself into influential circles.

Fergie, as a Boar, is natural, kindly, friendly, outgoing and personable. She works hard and plays hard, loving parties. She is also modest and happy to take a back seat in life, the kind of person that others are inclined to take for granted. She will devote herself to the people she loves and expects little in return, and is devoted to work and family. She will be able to shrug off criticism and won't look too far into the future. Famed for her patience, she will pursue her objective unstintingly until she attains it.

The Rat husband and the Boar wife will have a very physical relationship, although, as they are both of a hasty temperament, they will have their share of arguments. They will need a definite base, of either home or children, to make them fulfilled.

Ideally the Rat should have the most fulfilling relationship with another one of the Positive signs, either Dragon or Monkey (like Koo Stark) rather than the Negative-stemmed and emotional Boar, Sheep or Rabbit. Yet the Rat and the Boar are not in conflict, so the Metal Rats, such as Adlai Stevenson and Lucretia Borgia, can live a happy and productive life with the Earth Boar, such as John D. Rockefeller and Humphrey Bogart. And, as the Chinese point out, from Earth we mine the Metal to till the Earth again.

By the charts of Middle Eastern astrology, Andrew was born at the very time the Sun went into Pisces, which shows the deep sensitivity he is sometimes at pains to hide. His Moon is in Scorpio, a sign denoting much strength and deep but usually suppressed feeling which, complicated by the conjunction of Mars and Saturn together in Capricorn, linked with this Moon in Scorpio, makes for further complexity of feeling. Mars and Saturn together in Capricorn indicate a considerable degree of uncertainty for which he might well have to compensate in different areas of his life.

The placing of Mercury in Pisces in Andrew's chart lends an interesting aspect of vulnerability in contrast to the outwardly powerful Leo rising and electric Uranus. This is the sort of chart which does not augur for a comfortable youth – there is too much disturbance caused by Uranus for there to be signs of serenity before middle-age.

In some ways, Andrew's is a very artistic and creative chart and it is interesting that Uranus, associated with photography, should feature so strongly. The prime need for someone with this combination of elements in their chart is to be in control; it is not tolerable for them to be out of control or to lose dignity. Such a person would be likely to start their own business in order to be their own boss. Being a public figure inevitably imposes restraints on self-expression and inclines the subject further towards retreat and evasion.

Leo rising means that Andrew must be king of his particular roost – no doubt Fergie will discover how best to deal with this royal ego, especially as on the plus side there is kingly generosity and not an ounce of meanness.

This sense of largesse makes Andrew a thoughtful and romantic lover; the kind of man who arrives home with roses after a row, who wines and dines his lover and offers weekends in Paris – in preference to talking through a disagreement or coming to terms with real pain and hurt. He is the sort of man to whom many women would be initially drawn, only to find that what they thought they had caught has somehow slipped their grasp. His attraction lies in the appeal of uncertainty that is covered by a confident, possibly boastful exterior. This lion is afraid of nothing except being himself.

Andrew will, if he allows it, be helped by Fergie to come to terms with himself. He will need to realise that there are many ways of being a real man, a real hero, that do not preclude his showing his sensitivity. The important thing for Andrew will be to discover how to reveal his feelings without jeopardising what he sees as his masculinity. It is interesting that Andrew's super-male image should in fact be a form of defence mechanism constructed to deter invasion of privacy. It is perhaps only when he is in love that Andrew has felt free to express his feelings, although, even in loving, he is likely to need to be in control.

Andrew's need to protect himself means that sometimes he will inflict hurt and not realise it. But now he has found the woman who can truly stand up to him. Such resolution may not always be easy for her, but this area of uncovering their true feelings is where the true work of their marriage will lie.

Fergie's chart is exactly right to assist Andrew grow emotionally and it seems that the way ahead for her, while not likely to be altogether easy, is blessed above all with an uncanny, almost telepathic, understanding.

Fergie's Moon is in Aries, her Sun in Libra in conjunction with Mars. If control is Andrew's byword, courage is Fergie's. Her every action is ruled by phenomenal energy and practicality. The astrologer who read this chart, ignorant of its subject, sensed a strong mother whose influence had been withdrawn at some stage. It seems that when Fergie was little she was very attached to a mother-figure who is somehow absent – there seems to have been very little time for this child. And there is a strong sense of family here, with a mother whose influence, but not presence, is very intrusive in the chart.

This unfulfilled need for closeness to a mother has resulted in an unusually absorbent sensitivity. She is hyper-aware of atmospheres and vibrations and has a great need to make everything all right for everyone. Her own sense of loss makes her acutely aware of other people's feelings – but here the positive aspect of the Arian Moon glows with a constant cheerfulness. Fergie's energy and commitment to others draws from her the ebullience which makes her such entertaining company.

The drawback for Fergie is that it is difficult for her to

have confidence in her own huge strength and energy since she is so aware of others and their needs. It is here that the stars show the heart of Fergie's conflict – her powerful, dominant Mars is mitigated and confused by a full twelfth-house Scorpio rising, Neptune in conjunction with Mercury and Neptune in wide conjunction with Mars.

Her Venus in conjunction with Pluto in Virgo makes her anxious to achieve a perfect love, a powerful passion, whilst Mars creates a need for power. Somewhere Fergie is looking for the relationship which will alter everything, transform her existence and fill it with meaning.

She would be more likely to put up with a difficult situation than to hurt someone – she has an unusually developed sense of caring. She is a giver, adventurous and uninhibited, an initiator whose energies are pushed outwards toward the world with a delightful generosity. A tension is created, however, when such a strong Mars (which governs Aries, housekeeper to Fergie's Moon) is pulled back and constrained by concern for others. This is someone who is almost afraid of her own energy.

It is vital that she should not be tied down, and essential that she be involved with work that uses her creative energies to the full. She is at her best as an initiator, although this is a person who will enjoy every minute and cumbersome detail if the cause is right. The more daring the risks involved, the happier Fergie will be since bravery is her touchstone. She has the right spirit for pioneering, high-risk expeditions and the courage essential for adventure. There is a sort of dauntless daring about Fergie which, with the sensitive longings which are the residue of her childhood, Andrew will have to try to understand – this will require thoughtfulness on his part, which may be difficult for him faced with the resilient and capable façade with which she disguises her dilemma.

At the moment they are attracted to each other's strengths. When they discover each other's weaknesses and vulnerability and help each other to recognise them, the union will have found its natural maturity. Their relationship now has the healthy glow of true friendship which requires no effort to sustain it.

Fergie's happy exterior also hides her need to be reassured about what she sees as her selfishness. It will be very important for Andrew not to feel intimidated by her energy and to recognise the sort of encouragement that Fergie needs; while it may seem that Fergie needs protection from nothing, he must realise that this is a manifestation of her own unease.

Her greatest strength is her sensitivity, her charm and her cheerfulness – without doubt there is a complicated blend of practical but intuitive intelligence here. At the moment Fergie's defence against criticism is to deflect attack with jokes and the sort of carefree attitude which prevents people from taking her too seriously. However, it may be that whilst the Aries in her will bluster through uncertainty, Scorpio rising will long to sit silently in the corner.

She is a woman whose hidden seriousness leads to action rather than talk – she will always be inclined to find practical solutions to any given problem. She is too restless a person to want an easy life, and her energy and concern are poised to find their natural focus. So far there has been no job or enterprise in her life which has provided the sort of challenge for which she has the capacity. It may be that marriage to Andrew will lead to a lifetime of duties which will provide her with just the outlets for her energy that she needs.

The composite effect of these two star signs is hopeful but not without difficulty – Andrew and Fergie are unquestionably suited to each other and, if they can recognise those areas where each needs encouragement, they will have a resoundingly happy and successful marriage. Their sexual compatibility is beyond doubt – and their enjoyment of each other one of the happiest aspects of their combined chart. Andrew's Moon in Fergie's ascendant and her Jupiter is one indicator of a loving, satisfying and fulfilling physical relationship. The strong presence of Scorpio

shared by both of them warns that jealousy and possessive-
ness will have to be guarded against.

What these two charismatic, volatile people have to offer
each other is the possibility of finding the proper balance
between their needs and their wants through each other,
and with each other. It is possible that what is deeply
repressed in both of them – Andrew's doubts about his
masculinity, Fergie's fear that she is too selfish – may take
years to realise in terms of their relationship. There is,
however, so much generosity indicated in their charts that
with the good temper, the sense of fun and – very important
for them – their undisputed sexual compatibility, it is
impossible to imagine them not overcoming each and every
difficulty with the realistic and good-humoured sensitivity
which will, in ten years' time, have become a recognisable
feature of their marriage.

CHRISTOPHER WARWICK

PRINCESS MARGARET

Written with the full co-operation of Princess
Margaret, this is the first authorised biography of one
of the most remarkable members of the Royal Family.
Drawing on numerous conversations with her, this
fascinating account gives the most authentic record
yet published of the Princess's private life and public
duties. Christopher Warwick dispels the media-
created legends and reveals – at last – the woman
glass-cased inside the Princess.

CORONET BOOKS

ALSO AVAILABLE FOM CORONET

		Anne Edwards	
☐	28447 1	Sonya: The Life of Countess Tolstoy	£3.95
☐	23024 X	Vivien Leigh	£2.50
		Dorothy Laird	
☐	19919 9	Queen Elizabeth: The Queen Mother	£3.95
		Elizabeth Longford	
☐	36374 6	Elizabeth R: A Biography	£2.95
		Christopher Warwick	
☐	35487 9	Princess Margaret	£2.25

All these books are available at your local bookshop or newsagent, or can be ordered direct from the publisher. Just tick the titles you want and fill in the form below.
Prices and availability subject to change without notice.

CORONET BOOKS, P.O. Box 11, Falmouth, Cornwall.

Please send cheque or postal order, and allow the following for postage and packing:

U.K. – 55p for one book, plus 22p for the second book, and 14p for each additional book ordered up to a £1.75 maximum.

B.F.P.O. and EIRE – 55p for the first book, plus 22p for the second book, and 14p per copy for the next 7 books, 8p per book thereafter.

OTHER OVERSEAS CUSTOMERS – £1.00 for the first book, plus 25p per copy for each additional book.

Name ....

Address ....

....

ANNE EDWARDS

SONYA: THE LIFE OF COUNTESS TOLSTOY

This is the sweeping human and profoundly moving portrait of an extraordinary woman caught in a tumultuous marriage to a man all the world regarded as a god. But in reality Tolstoy was cruel, selfish and neglectful, preferring to channel his energies into his literary genius rather than towards his devoted wife. Sonya's story is as exciting as that of any novel her husband wrote, a love story of tremendous intensity and passion which will enthral the reader to the very last page.

POSTAL LITTLE HAPPINESS

Post·A·Book

A Royal Mail service in association with the Book Marketing Council & The Booksellers Association.

Post-A-Book is a Post Office trademark.

ANNE EDWARDS

VIVIEN LEIGH

The story of how she won the coveted role of Scarlett
O'Hara from a host of celebrated screen actresses
became a Hollywood legend. Churchill, Coward,
Gielgud and Brando were just a few of the glittering
people who surrounded her. But behind the dazzling
exterior lay the sinister shadow of a second Vivien
Leigh – a shadow which pursued her throughout her
aristocratic upbringing, her frustrating first marriage,
her tempestuous romance with Laurence Olivier and
her meteoric rise to stardom.

CORONET BOOKS